DEALING WITH DIFFICULT PEOPLE

CHARLES J. KEATING

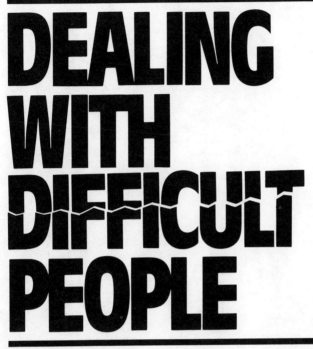

DEALING WITH DIFFICULT PEOPLE

HOW *YOU* CAN COME OUT ON TOP IN PERSONALITY CONFLICTS

PAULIST PRESS **NEW YORK/RAMSEY**

Library of Congress
Catalog Card Number: 83-82018

ISBN: 0-8091-2596-X

Published by Paulist Press
545 Island Road, Ramsey, N.J. 07446

Printed and bound in the
United States of America

Contents

To
My sister, Helen
She is *not* one of my difficult people

Introduction

Difficulties are like ocean froth: they can demand your total attention or you can choose to look beyond, to the vast tranquillity of the sea. The further view does not do away with the froth, but it places it in perspective.

While the title may not indicate it, this is a happy book. It is a book of hope. It says that difficult things need not remain difficult. We are in a society that tries to explain away difficulties. We are not supposed to be upset or disturbed by them. In fact, we are not supposed to recognize problems or difficulties. They are supposed to be challenges! Substituting "challenges" for "difficulties," I think, is a destructive euphemism. Real people have real difficulties. They shrivel, retreat and even die because of difficulties. People kill people without ever being brought "to justice." We kill the "spirit" of another, the "confidence of another," and we kill careers. The world is poorer because of the talents we have sacrificed to fear, ambition and financial security. Few "successful" people will question that reality. They have "survived." They know many who have not. The purpose of this book is to reduce the number of non-survivors and to increase the number of the successful.

Successful people might still need to read what follows, lest they become victims of "difficulties." Surviving "people-eaters" lasts as long as we are financially dependent upon others. Perhaps longer. We can still find "difficulty" within the family and with friends, long after we are financially independent. It is a human condition, it seems.

My personal experience, the shared experiences of my relatives and friends, the Sunday newspaper (we do not take the daily paper), and my professional experience as a consultant and trainer in human relationships and organization development led me to write about "difficulties." They seem to be pervasive, found everywhere we turn. They probably are uni-

1

versal, if the world situation as reported to us has any validity. For twenty years I worked in an international organization. I found a good number of difficulties, some of which I, no doubt, created. My wife, an affable, hard-working person, has worked in three organizations over a period of ten years. As time went on in each organization, I have had to accept her return home each evening ready to "fight," "bite," and/or "erupt." She had left each morning with hope and enthusiasm. In each job, she liked her work. She found difficulty with people. Perhaps she contributed the difficulty, but we shall talk about that, also, in this book. I'm prejudiced, so I think it was the fault of others! But . . .? What happened at work took a toll on our marriage. It is not what it was when she did not have to work. We have had to use all of the skills of this book to remain married and together. There is no lack of love, only an intrusion of "difficulty."

Too long, it seems to me, have we denied the pleasure of life and the satisfaction of being human. We introduce "difficulty," and make misery. The poet, Coventry Patmore, has expressed how we miss the point:

> How long shall men deny the flower
>   Because its roots are in the earth,
> And crave with tears from God the dower
>   They have, and have despised as dearth,
> And scorn as low their human lot,
>   With frantic pride, too blind to see
> That standing on the head makes not
>   Either for ease or dignity!
> But fools shall feel like fools to find
>   (Too late inform'd) that angels' mirth
> Is one in cause, and mode, and kind
>   With that which they profaned on earth.

Difficulties are the things that we do to each other that make life unpleasant. They are the situations into which we fall, or into which we are pushed, that make us uncomfortable. They are people with whom we choose to relate and situations in which we choose to be that disappoint us and present problems. They are part of the human condition. If we did not have them, we would be in heaven, not on earth. Patmore's point is that we take them too seriously. But, perhaps, we must. There will be time for mirth, later.

Difficulties are as complex and varied as human nature. We have "personality clashes" that include the personality with which we are born and the styles of interpersonal relationships that we learn "from our mother's knee." We view such differences as difficulties, until we may perceive the value of differences. Maybe we can see differences as useful. Chapter 1 explores such a possibility.

The "games" of Transactional Analysis create serious difficulties for all of us, especially since we play them unconsciously. In Chapter 2 we expose them for what they are, analyze their dynamics and suggest ways to short-circuit them.

Most of the day-to-day difficulties we experience focus on a one-to-one situation. They often arise from our assumptions about ourselves and about others. We assume too much or too little. In Chapter 3 we have the opportunity to "test" the effects of our assumptions.

There are difficulties we find at home and at work, each having their own characteristics and sets of dynamics. We consider such specifics in Chapters 4 and 5. Marriage difficulties can occasion job difficulties and job difficulties can create marriage problems. We do not live in boxes. Our world is our "box" where we find ourselves related to home and job, needing to accept the fact that we carry about all of our relationships within ourselves, as a bird must find work and family in the nest. We are made up of a series of semipermeable membranes that allow all that we are and all that we experience to flow together and to mix.

For a few of us, the gifted intellectuals perhaps, difficulties are cognitive. They consist of frustrating formulas or abortive research experiments. Feelings may be secondary in such experiences. For most of us, feelings are paramount, supplying difficulties with their strength and direction. In Chapter 6 we reflect on the power of feelings, new thinking about handling feelings and how feelings relate to the difficulties we experience. Ninety percent of our difficulties are rooted in feelings, and feelings touch our total person. My experience with group training has been that most of us are not aware of our feelings. If we are not aware of them, we cannot handle them. The majority of people I have trained in leadership skills and group dynamics do not know how to express (or how not to express) feelings in a constructive way. Over the last twelve years I have trained more than ten thousand people. I have no reason to believe that the majority of these people were any more proficient in expressing and handling feelings one-on-one than they were in expressing and handling feelings within a group situation. We take ourselves with us, no matter where we go.

In many ways, handling difficulties and the accompanying feelings in a group is less of a challenge than handling difficulties and feelings person-to-person. Chapter 7 reflects on ways to prevent difficulties from arising in groups. A working knowledge of group development and group expectations goes far toward smooth and effective group satisfaction and productivity. I also suggest ways to handle group difficulties when they occur.

Confrontation is a classic tactic for handling difficulty. We explore ways to do it and the importance of our mind set when we confront in Chapter 8. I shall also suggest alternatives to confrontation and situations in which confrontation may not be useful for resolving difficulties.

Chapter 9 is a brief reflection on the larger arena of difficulty. We focus on difficult life change: divorce, separation, widowhood, job change, career change and retirement. Of the many difficulties we face in life, life change, whether chosen or imposed, is the most demanding, because it touches the very fabric of our lives. It affects the closest of our relationships, our most intimate dreams and the heart of our being. It touches our soul and spirit. None of us take such difficulty lightly, although we may pretend and seem to do so.

Difficulties can eat us alive. Some statistics indicate that for every one percent of unemployment, a difficult life change, there are nine hundred suicides. We know that submitting is not the answer. By submitting to difficulty, either by suicide or hopeless resignation, we only multiply the difficulty. We suffer more and those closest to us suffer more. All of us lose.

There is a better way. It only needs the lights of understanding and appreciation. To turn the switches, read on.

1

Differences and Difficulties

Mary was a difficult person. She managed the fashion department of our business with efficiency and success, so that while other departments failed to meet expectations and quotas Mary's department never faltered. I met her the second day on the job and felt almost a chemical repulsion: she was brisk, uninterested and uninteresting. I received the impression that I wasn't worth spending time or energy on; she had better things to do. After being transferred to her department my impression did not change. She rarely said "thank you," only on the most unusual occasions did she ask my opinion, and she never said "I made a mistake." She seemed to know everything I told her before I told her! It was unpleasant working with her. She was a difficult person.

Most of us have met difficult people, people that we find it hard to relate to in a satisfying manner: the person we just cannot "figure out," the chronic complainer who seems to have little to complain about, the "one-upper" who always needs to go you one better, the "cold fish," and the hundreds of other types we could name. Then, we think, "Maybe it's my fault. I just don't understand him. Maybe it's me!"

And that might be true. The key to coping with difficult people, the secret of maintaining our own tranquillity in a stormy or unpleasant relationship, frequently is understanding ourselves and why we respond the way we do. Socrates did give us good advice when he said "Know yourself" nearly twenty-five hundred years ago.

But it can't always be me, unless I'm a difficult person myself! But if you are always at fault, if you are the difficult person

7

about whom this book is written, you probably wouldn't be reading this book in the first place. Difficult people rarely feel they need help in dealing with others. That's part of what makes them difficult.

When I was on a college faculty I found that those faculty members who needed help in relating to students and fellow faculty most seriously, those faculty members who seemed most unhappy, were the last to accept opportunities for help. They had erected great impregnable walls around themselves; they vibrated hostility and self-righteousness. One teacher regularly belittled students in public, even though he had been warned by the dean about this behavior time and again. He was safe, because he was tenured. He was also difficult. Human relation workshops never saw his face; relaxed dialogue was a stranger to his experience. Students called him "The Dragon," and not affectionately. "The Dragon" felt no need for help.

So, if you're reading this book, chances are that you are not among the difficult people I am writing about. This is not to say that we all should ignore Socrates, for we can contribute to and even compound the "difficulty" we find in difficult people with our own attitude and behavior. Learning about ourselves is part, but only part, of learning to handle difficult people. Learning what makes them difficult is the larger part of the answer we seek.

Personality Conflicts

One of the easiest ways to "write off" a person with whom we are having a difficulty is to attribute the difficulty to a "difference in personality." And the fact that this is an easy write-off doesn't make it wrong. There might well be a personality difference that creates the conflict. What makes our write-off wrong is that it is a write-off, allowing for no solution. It doesn't go far enough. Personality conflicts can be handled by understanding, tolerating and eventually appreciating basic personality differences. Differences can be enrichments rather than conflicts.

According to many psychologists each one of us is born with a basic, bedrock personality. With experience we add on to that personality, develop skills and learn information that can enrich that basic personality, but it never really changes. We are who we are at the age of six months, six years and sixty years. If we are born an extravert we shall die an extravert; if we are born a thinker, we shall die a thinker. Contrary to popular notions, personality cannot be changed, shed or crushed. It can only go into hiding when necessary, especially when survival is at stake.

Isabel Briggs Myers spent more than forty years building upon the personality constructs of Carl Jung. She concluded that our basic personality is made up of a mix of extraversion, introversion, sensing, intuition, feeling, thinking, judging and perceiving. Her theory is the foundation of the Myers-Briggs Personality Type Indicator.

While it might be true in physics that "opposites attract," it is not so true in human relationships. We tend to feel most comfortable with those of the same personality as ourselves. I worked closely with a man for two years before I knew anything of Isabel Briggs Myers. I liked him and felt very close to him at times; at other times I felt quite alienated from him but did not know why. When both of us came upon the Personality Indicator we discovered that I was a strong introvert, while he was on the borderline between introversion and extraversion. As we reflected back over our experience, we found that my feelings of closeness seemed to occur when he was behaving as an introvert; my feelings of alienation arose when he acted as an extravert. At such times, I felt left out and abandoned, disappointed to the point that I felt the loss of a friend.

Jeremiah, an associate of mine, is an introvert. Contrary to the popular understanding of "introverts," he is not a wallflower or recluse; in fact, he is well liked, popular and successful in his interpersonal relationships. His recent award as "Salesman of the Year" testifies to his success with people. But it does take time to know Jeremiah; he is not what he appears to be when you meet him. He seems warm, feeling and approachable. And he is. But most of all he likes to be inside his own head; he is most himself when inside himself, a person not impacted by others. But you have to know Jeremiah a bit before you realize where his interests and first love lie. He isn't being deceitful; he is not lying or playing games; he is simply being an introvert. A major characteristic of the introvert is that upon first meeting "what you see is not what you get." Their basic personality requires that they share with you only the less important part of their personality until they develop some kind of trusting relationship with you. By nature they "introvert" what is most important to them.

Sometimes people believe that Jeremiah's behavior is devious, or at least confusing. It does create problems for him, problems he does not always understand: "Why are they upset?" "What ticked her off?" and "What happened?" are common questions that Jeremiah asks himself. Jeremiah's friend has told me that she spends half of her life explaining him to other people!

Another characteristic of Jeremiah, the introvert, is that he needs time to make the transition from one kind of situation to another, from one task to another; he does not appear too flexible. If I give an urgent job to Amy and to Jeremiah at the same time, Amy is halfway through the job before Jeremiah is ready to begin. Amy is an extravert. Jeremiah cannot change gears so readily. Because he is most himself when he is in his own head, he tends to become totally immersed in the job at hand; if he is programming the computer, he will be programming it for an hour or so after the job is complete. He needs that hour before moving into a new and different task, such as writing copy for a newsletter. Amy can be programming the computer one minute and be well into writing copy the next. Jeremiah isn't lazy or stubborn; he just functions differently than an extravert like Amy.

Personal life is also affected by personality differences of introversion and extraversion. Both Amy and Jeremiah drive an hour from their workplace to their homes. Amy, upon entering the front door, is ready for love, even though she worked on the computer all day; Jeremiah is not. He needs time to adapt anew to the home and hearth, so different from the computer and the work world. To avoid unnecessary conflict, Jeremiah's family needs to "leave him alone" for a while. This is not to say that everyone doesn't need time to make transitions and to be alone on occasion. It is to say that introverts seem to need such time as a normal pattern. Neither is it to say that Jeremiah's behavior may very well indicate a lazy or rigid character trait. I am saying that we need to understand something of the other person before we allow his or her behavior to cause conflict, with ourselves or with others. Suspicion, attributing malice where there is none, negative evaluations and "why can't he be like me" thinking are major causes of conflict. We can make another a difficult person, and, in turn, become difficult ourselves.

Amy and Jeremiah are very much alike in most situations. Under pressure, however, they differ. Amy immediately moves to handle the conflict or tension: she will be diplomatic, aggressive/assertive or withdraw as she judges to be best. Jeremiah will always first withdraw, taking time to evaluate the situation and the best means to calm the storm. To Amy he appears to be sulking, and she may resent this. But again, Jeremiah is acting like an introvert while Amy is acting like an extravert. Additional conflict can build on the tension unless personality differences are at least tolerated, if not appreciated.

Another example of personality conflict, following the categories of Myers-Briggs, is the difference between the sensing personality and the intuitive personality. Each gathers information about the world and the situation in which they live in a very different way. Joan is a sensing personality. She is attentive to detail, aware of color, light and shadings in her physical surroundings. The first thing she did when she walked into her new office was to notice the color the walls were painted, the carpet on the floor and the coverings for the windows. Her boss values her for her grasp of the fine print in contracts and for her practical turn of mind. Joan has contact with her surroundings like no other personality type. She is always present in the present.

Vivian, Joan's boss, is an intuitive. True, she values Joan, but she also finds her somewhat of a bore; she doesn't enjoy socializing with Joan, although she doesn't know what she would do without her in the office. An intuitive is a dreamer and a conceptualizer, a person whose main concern is about the implications of an idea or a situation. An intuitive is never quite present in the present; he or she is always looking to the future and to what the implications of the present are for the future. To Vivian, Joan is a bore because she is satisfied with the ways things are, or if she isn't, Joan can't imagine what to do about it in any original way. To Joan, Vivian is a mystery. "How did she ever get to be vice president with so little attention to detail?" As an intuitive, which has nothing to do with "women's intuition" or ESP, Vivian probably is not aware that half of the walls of her office are paneled in white oak or that her carpet is a navy blue. To her, such details are not important; the implications of what she and the company are doing is important; the significance of her luncheon date this afternoon is important; it is the future that is important.

Without Joan, Vivian would be likely to make a number of errors: she does not like to read the fine print, look at the nitty gritty details of a plan or be bothered with everyday items. Along the way, she will very likely be "tripped up" by her ignoring of detail. That's where she needs Joan. But she doesn't really like Joan; she only "values her."

Recently Vivian fought long and hard for the expansion of her training facilities. Headquarters was difficult to convince that extended facilities would result in a better "bottom line." Miraculously, in Vivian's view, the president had agreed that increased facilities, more meeting rooms, dining facilities and sleeping space, would benefit the company in the long run, at the "bottom line." She returned to her office jubilant! She couldn't wait to share the news with someone—and Joan was there.

She shared with Joan. "But will the boilers handle the increased heating demand? You'll have to hire more maintenance people! How about the rest rooms? Won't more be needed?" Vivian was crushed. Vivian was already planning the new programs that increased facilities would accommodate, the multiple numbers of people her programs could touch. Joan was a "wet blanket," a "kill-joy."

Vivian became depressed; Joan couldn't understand why. The seeds of conflict were sown. In enthusiasm, neither recognized the strengths of the other. Vivian needed Joan to be realistic and practical; Joan needed Vivian to "get out of the rut" and to move into new pastures. Each was an invaluable asset to the other, but neither recognized it.

In the executive offices another conflict was burgeoning: the financial vice president couldn't understand why the president had given Vivian permission to expand the training facility. Joseph, the financial vice president, was a thinker. He made judgments in the light of logic, reason and practicality. John, the president, had listened to Vivian and saw her enthusiasm, drive and commitment. John is a "feeler," making decisions from his "guts," his feelings for others and his own feelings.

As a "thinker" personality type, Joseph seemed to be cold, indifferent and insensitive to the ideas of others; he may have appeared superior, unwilling to repeat ideas already expressed and reluctant to explain himself. John felt he was this way. But Joseph had found success in his approach. He had become a vice president! What he said was reasonable; he couldn't understand the resistance. What he said made sense from a logical point of view. In Joseph's viewpoint, people too often tried to create their own kingdoms. He was there to keep the company logical and reasonable. Employees, vice presidents or managers, had to recognize the financial logistics of the company!

John, the president, was a "feeler." He made decisions from his "guts": his own feelings and his sensitivity to the feelings of others. Vivian, seated before him, was feeling deeply: she wanted more room to do her job; she had come to him to ask for it. John's feelings were "to help." He felt for her, and he made his decision out of that feeling.

John may be unfair, supporting Vivian while other needs,

not immediately before him, go untended; but that is the weakness of the "feeler." Joseph may be confused, uncertain why he meets such opposition when he is so reasonable. Each personality type has its limitations, and, therefore, its need of its opposite.

Vivian and Joan, John and Joseph need each other! According to the forty years of research done by Myers-Briggs, all of us have a little of Vivian and Joan, a little of John and Joseph in us: but one or the other trait usually predominates.

Meanwhile, in the marketing and sales departments another personality "conflict" was brewing. Don, director of marketing, is a "judging" personality. This does not mean that he is judgmental or that he feels compelled to be the conscience of the company. As a "judger," Don likes order and is most comfortable with schedule and clear expectations. Even on Saturday morning he is a bit uncomfortable if he doesn't know how he will spend the afternoon. At work Don likes to know what is expected of him, how he is expected to work and when projects are to be begun and concluded. He is least happy with the unexpected and unplanned. He is most comfortable when he controls life.

Martha, director of sales, is different. She is most comfortable when she can simply live life. She accepts planning and scheduling as necessary evils in the life of the corporation; she would prefer to allow things to happen and handle them as they do. She is good at that. She had been successful with such behavior all of her life. Things got done, jobs were accomplished well without the rigidity of planning and order. She is good in a crisis and an emergency. Martha is seen as flexible and easy-going.

But Don doesn't see Martha that way. Since he has to work closely with sales, he is frequently upset by the "disorder" of the department. He even suspects that Martha might be lazy, incompetent or "not too bright." Last week he suggested that the two departments sit down for some integrated planning sessions, so that there would be fewer crises and, in Don's view, smoother operations. He is still waiting to hear from Martha.

Martha has a "perceiving" personality. As a "perceiver," she tends to feel restricted and even bored by scheduling and order. Don is simply too military-like in her view: "He'd have us all running around like robots if he could," she has been heard to say. When she has been more irritated than usual, her closest friends have heard her proclaim, "I'll bet Don has scheduled his own death!" Martha sees the need for some order and routine in a business, but rigid planning just seems to go *too* far. "Leave some room to be human," she often says.

The conflict of personalities between Don and Martha erupts periodically, but especially as each new fiscal year approaches. Then Don is most pressing for commonly agreed goals, detailed objectives and time schedules. Martha feels most uncomfortable at this time: the "stuff" has to be done, but "you can't plan everything!" Martha and Don don't get along well! They see it as a "personality clash."

Without a doubt, there are personality "clashes" and "conflicts" that arise from a basic, almost inborn, preference each of us has of the way we like to live life, to work and to behave. At least, this is one conclusion reached by research done with the Myers-Briggs Personality Type instruments. They are clashes that can be most serious and disruptive precisely because they are unconscious preferences, likes and dislikes that arise from the partially hidden self in each one of us. We frequently don't understand the source of the stress and conflict, and we too often "write it off" as an insoluble personality clash.

Jeremiah and Amy, Joan and Vivian, John and Joseph, and Don and Martha could capitalize on their strengths! Each had something the other did not; each had something to offer the other. Jeremiah had reflection and a sense of tranquillity, not affected by the "outside world"; Amy had flexibility and openness, and she had honest reactions to a situation. Joan had a grasp of detail and a sensibility to reality while Vivian could have helped to see what lay ahead, consequences and possibilities. John felt for people; he was responsive to their needs and masterful at keeping people in the company. Joseph kept the company viable, a master at facing the real world of demand and accountability. Don helped to make the company aware of the importance of planning for the future, while Martha was "on the spot" ready to handle problems as they arose.

John Donne, the poet, wrote many years ago that "no man is an island." His reflection was never truer than in the hidden world of personality. Each personality type needs the other. Each of us has assets that reveal an unknown world to the other. It is as though each of us has blinders, hiding from us the other side of reality. Since this blindness is congenital, we cannot overcome it without the help of others. There are some of us who can see both sides, and usually we are most confusing to our associates. When they think they have us "down pat" they become upset when we behave differently than they expect. Those of us like that are generally on the borderline between extravert and introvert, intuitive and sensing, feeling and thinking, or perceiving and judging. Even this balance can be a source of conflict. Such conflict usually emerges within ourselves; we cannot understand why people behave to us the way they do.

I once lived with a man who was on the borderline between introversion and extraversion. The time was long before I had heard of Myers-Briggs or personality types. I am an introvert. When my friend was introverted, I felt close to him; I felt I had a friend. When he was extraverted, I felt excluded and alienated; I saw him as a stranger. In spite of the old adage that "opposites attract," we like to be with our own. We are most comfortable with those of our own personality type.

But comfort and success are not easy bedfellows. We may not be comfortable with the personality type that we need most. The introvert sees the extravert as superficial and the extravert sees the introvert as brooding. The intuitive sees the sensing as boring and pessimistic, while the sensing sees the intuitive as a dreamer or a malcontent. The feeler perceives the thinker as insensitive and hard, and the thinker views the feeler as an emotional blob and "soft-touch." The perceiver ranks the judger as rigid and "unnecessary," while the judger considers the perceiver as lazy or incompetent. There is no doubt that the seeds of personality clash are built in from birth or near birth. If each baby is different, so is each person.

We have seen examples of different personality types and caught glimpses of possible conflicts. We need to review briefly those eight elements of the Myers-Briggs categories to clear our minds.

Introverts: most at home in their own heads. They can be very personable and charming, but these are learned skills, as with everyone. They are most themselves when they are by themselves or with an intimate friend. They do not readily reveal their true selves to others. They need time to grow in trust with another; they need time to make a transition from one external situation to another. In stress, they will first withdraw to consider the situation and the proper response.

Extraverts: most at home with others. They are what they seem to be when you meet them. There are no secrets they unconsciously withhold. They enjoy being with others and sometimes find it difficult to be alone. Like the introvert, the extravert can be charming with others if he or she has learned the skills. The extravert will readily handle a stressful situation and readily make the transition from one situation to another, even though the situations are quite different.

Sensing: in contact with reality like no other personality type. They are nitty-gritty people, paying attention to the small print, very aware of the physical surroundings, attentive to detail and very practical. They tend to be loyal to an institution or corporation, responsive to the problems of managers or superiors and good followers if they feel they are appreciated.

Intuitives: the conceptualizers and dreamers of the organization. They tend to see possibilities rather than realities. Intuitives weigh everything in terms of what it means, rather than in terms of its present consequences. They like to plan, to organize and to make relationships not readily seen by others. If they are not disciplined, they may seem to be cranks or malcontents. They are anxious to try the new and the different. More than other personality types, they like to write books and formulate theories.

Thinkers: tend to see all in the light of reason and logic. While they may or may not score high on IQ, they value the intellect and reasonable thinking above all. They are cognitive. They view emotions of themselves or of others as of secondary importance, more of a problem than as part of a solution. Their decisions often do not take into account the feelings of others, so that they do not understand why others react the way they do.

Feelers: make decisions from their "guts," how they feel and the way they "think" others are feeling. They tend to be warm and approachable, open to the "opinions" and feelings of others. Feelers are sometimes blind to logic and reason, deciding in terms of the pain they or others are feeling. They can be unjust, making decisions in favor of those before them to the detriment to those not present. But they do not do this intentionally; it is their "blind spot."

Perceivers: live life as it is; they feel comfortable with the "happening" or the "crisis," and do not need to have things scheduled or in order. They are content to "drink in" the situation, without feeling the need to make any decisions or conclusions about it. They can take day by day, without feeling the need of a plan or specific purpose.

Judgers: need to control life; they are most comfortable with order and schedule, knowing what to expect of others as well as of themselves. While they may not savor routine, they do like schedule and feel a bit of discomfort when the unexpected confronts them. They find it difficult to function well in an atmosphere they perceive as disordered. They can be flexible if they understand that this is expected of them.

Little reflection is needed to imagine the conflicts that can arise from the interaction of these elements of personality. We have already seen some examples of likely conflicts. But if we accept the findings of Myers-Briggs research, the possibilities of conflict reach infinity. According to that research, each of us shares in four of the above elements to a preeminent degree: each of us is either predominantly introvert *or* extravert, intuitive *or* sensing, feeling *or* thinking, perceiving *or* judging. Personality clash can occur at several levels. They are real—but they can be understood!

More important, differences in personality can be appreciated, or, at least, tolerated. With a little reflection, it becomes obvious to us that intuitives need what sensing personalities have to offer, if they are not to trip over the *facts* that are right in front of them but to which they are blind. Sensing personalities need intuitives if they are not to remain unchanged, doing the same things over and over when such things could be done differently and, perhaps, better. Sensing personalities need the "possibilities" offered by the intuitive.

When making decisions, feelers need thinkers if they are not to be unfair and unjust; thinkers need feelers if they are not to be bewildered by the reception their decisions receive. Feelers tend to respond to the plight of those in front of them, or to respond to their own "gut" feelings. They may make decisions without those in mind who are "out-of-sight." That could be unjust. The "out-of-sight" people could have their rights neglected simply because the feeler is thinking only of the need of those present or of himself or herself. Thinkers risk upsetting others by ignoring the feelings of others. Their decisions might be crisp and reasonable, but they need to recognize that those decisions affect real people with feelings and unreasonable drives. People are not "brains on stilts"; they encompass fear, anxiety, hope, anger and love. Thinkers run the risk of speaking only to the brain. If, as we are often told, "people are our most important asset," thinkers, without conferring with feelers on major decisions, risk "our most valuable asset." Feelers, without conferring with thinkers on major decisions, risk being unjust, unfair to "our most valuable asset."

It seems clear to me that intuitives need sensing personalities and sensing personalities need intuitive personalities and that thinkers need feelers and feelers need thinkers. Rather than conflict with one another, we complement each other. We may be more comfortable with our own "kind," but our own "kind" may not be the best for us. Beyond toleration, we need to appreciate opposites.

The need is less clear when we speak of introverts and extraverts, but even here personality "clashes" may be softened by understanding. If the extravert accepts the introvert as naturally "more closed," as withdrawn in the face of conflict and as slow to make transitions, a "clash" is less likely. If the introvert can appreciate the extravert's openness, accept the readiness of the extravert to tackle conflict and make transitions, conflict may erupt more rarely. Mutual understanding is less a matter of compromise and indulgence than it is of appreciation and valuing differences.

Perceivers do have need of judgers and judgers of perceivers, but, again, this need is less clear; more important is that each accept the other for what the other is. The judger is valuable for the creation of order and organization; the perceiver is valuable for the "moment of crisis" and for handling the unexpected. The judger can "steamroll" the perceiver by taking over tasks the perceiver is expected to do, and thereby "one-up" the perceiver; the judger then has to be ready to handle the perceiver's anger and resentment. The perceiver can frustrate the judger simply by "laying back," by ignoring the concerns of the judger. Then both are losers. Clashes can be avoided if each appreciates the other's basic preferences and strengths and utilizes or, better, values them. Each has his or her moment in time and place.

Personality clashes seem to be inevitable; it would be worse if we did not risk them. If all of us were the same, all of us would be missing half of reality; we would be the blind leading the blind. It seems that we have been born to see and to handle about half or more of reality. Unless we are among those few who can easily switch from one view to another, we tend to see only half of what is in front of us. We can learn skills to broaden our horizon, as we shall see in Chapter 6, but we still prefer to see only half of the whole. Those whom we view as "difficult people" may be very valuable assets to us, seeing what we do not. And we may be valuable assets to them.

SURVIVAL STRATEGIES

1. Don't let yourself be upset when a "difficult person" responds or approaches you in ways that you yourself would not. Don't judge others by your own preferences.
2. You probably cannot change the basic personality of another. It is better to work toward appreciating what the other has to offer that complements your own personality. Don't try to change people unless they ask for your help in changing themselves.
3. In your head, never aloud, analyze before you react to another: "What is his or her frame of reference?" "Can a basic personality characteristic help explain the other's behavior?" "Can a basic personality characteristic help explain *my own* inclination to react in a particular way?" "Can I react in my favorite way, or would it be more appropriate to use one of my less favorite personality traits?"
4. Use your less favored personality type if it is appropriate to handling the difficulty. Use your "Sensing," for instance, if you favor "Intuition," when "Sensing" will help you get on the other's "wavelength." You will not feel as comfortable in your secondary preference, but practicing our auxiliary processes is actually good for us. Becoming stronger in our auxiliary process helps us to grasp a fuller picture of reality.
5. Keep in mind that not all interpersonal conflict is due solely to personality differences. Mary, the first example in this chapter, is a "Thinker"; she values efficiency and logic above people. I am a "Feeler," so there is some friction between Mary and me. But Mary also seems insecure to me, an acquired trait not explained by basic personality preferences. This compounds the difficulty. In addition to being a Thinker Mary cannot admit to making a mistake or to lacking information. Recognize such multiple levels of complexity as "Mary's problem." Stay detached. Don't get caught up in another's "problem" and don't make it your own.
6. On the other hand, where we find difficulty arising from acquired traits, such as feelings of insecurity or fear of closeness, we may survive best by being complimentary and

supportive of the good qualities we find in the other. These are indirect, non-threatening approaches that can eliminate difficulties if pursued consistently and sincerely.

7. Don't use basic personality types to label people, saying, for instance, "Well, what do you expect from an introvert?" That only creates difficulty. Use the types for your own better understanding, but don't cast them in concrete. They are tools, not weapons.

Interpersonal Relationship Difficulties

So far we have only touched the tip of the iceberg of "difficult people." No doubt there are natural personality differences that can create problems for us. But we do not function on nature alone; along the way each of us has learned forms of behavior that we have evaluated as more or less successful in dealing with people and with situations. Such patterns began in our homes, were modified in our school social life and carried into our own work and family life. Patterns we found successful were repeated and became "part of ourselves"; patterns that were not successful we discarded.

Patterns that we perceive as "part of ourselves" are not always successful. Because we believe they are part of our make-up we continue to repeat them. But there may come a time or a place when they are no longer successful: we are confused about the reactions of others to our behavior; we feel an emptiness in our own lives; if we are fortunate, our friends tell us that we are confusing to them. We then become "difficult people"; more, those who experience such confusion become difficult people to us. They too might be repeating previously successful behavior that is no longer successful. We do this unconsciously because we have learned unconsciously. We do not purposefully choose to act in a particular way in each situation; we act that way because it has been successful before. Our behavior is often "second nature," but because, unlike personality type, it is not "nature" it can be changed.

Thelma is a great party giver. She likes to arrange fun gatherings for her friends. Last Christmas she invited a number of friends to her home for a surprise party. The "surprise" was that all gifts had their tags removed, the gifts were shuffled and everyone received "pot-luck" from Thelma in her Santa Claus outfit. In the end, everyone had fun, as Thelma had planned. Since then Thelma has not accepted invitations from her friends, even to dinner or to a movie, except on rare occasions. Friends have begun to see her as "difficult" or, as some friends described it, as "weird."

Thelma liked to *include* people in her life and interests; she was not very interested in *being included* in the lives or interests of others. She had found success with this pattern in the past. She frequently initiated social or work gatherings, calling people to respond to her fun or work needs, but she rarely responded to the invites of others. Fellow workers found that she did not ordinarily respond to their requests for shared decision making sessions or workshops on departmental integration.

William Schutz, about forty years ago, was requested by the U.S. Navy to construct an instrument that would help them assemble compatible submarine crews, groups of men who could live together, elbow to elbow, for extended periods of time with minimum conflict among themselves. Schutz set out to assemble those qualities and characteristics that most influenced interpersonal behavior. After much research and experimentation he arrived at about thirty-two such qualities, far too many to include in a simple instrument destined for wide use. He settled for the three most significant behavior patterns that determine our interpersonal effectiveness: *inclusion, control* or influence and *affect.* The example of Thelma illustrates something of inclusion.

Inclusion refers to the level at which we like to include people in our lives and the level at which we like to be included in the lives of others. Our preference can range from choosing to live our lives in closeness to a very few to living in a way that includes many in our lives and interests; also, we can choose to become close to only a few to becoming close to many at their invitation. Inclusion measures the breadth and the depth of the friends we choose and accept. Thelma liked to choose her friends, and she chose widely; she called them to herself. She did not like being chosen, so she often refused invitations from those who accepted her own invitations. Her behavior was confusing to her "friends," and Thelma felt the consequences. Soon her invitations were rejected and she received fewer and fewer herself. She saw her "friends" as difficult and they saw her as difficult. The learned pattern of inclusion Thelma had once found successful was no longer so. And she couldn't understand why.

Sid, a colleague of mine and a university professor, did not have the same difficulty. He responded to invitations as readily as he gave them, which was seldom. He was considered, and accepted, as somewhat of a clique person. Sid's confusing behavior emanated from "control." A member of the board of directors of a small corporation, Sid was a question mark to his fellow directors. Without reason, he seemed to be highly influencing on one occasion and, without reason, seemed to be highly docile on another occasion. Some thought he had hidden interests on one or the other occasion, but this did not prove to be true. He simply vacillated between being highly controlling and being highly docile. No one knew where he stood. But Sid had found this behavior successful in the past. He was not trying to be mysterious or confusing; he was simply repeating successful behavior. His behavior relating to inclusion was clear: he was selective. His behavior relating to control was unpredictable and, therefore, confusing.

Control refers to the level at which we behave as an influencing person *and* the level at which we behave in a docile manner and are willing to be influenced by others. If we are clearly influencing, a kind of "take-charge" person, people know where we stand; if we are clearly willing to be influenced, a docile person, people also feel comfortable with us, perceiving us as predictable. Like Sid, we seem to have a problem when we are not predictable, when we are influencing on one occasion and docile on another. What creates the problem for others, and ultimately for ourselves since we may be confused by the reaction of others, is that there seems to be no apparent reason for our behavior on one or the other occasion. If there is a reason, such as vested interests we have that are known to others, or the situation is such that it requires a less docile posture, our differing behavior is often not a problem: we are simply acting in ways that make sense and fill the needs of a particular situation. The problem arises when we are controlling or non-controlling in a habitual fashion that seems without conscious intent. In the next chapter we shall see how we sometimes seek to control others unconsciously by playing "Games," as described by Eric Berne, the creator of the theory of Transactional Analysis.

Some ways Sid controlled were by reading magazines during meetings, by a game called "Kick Me," or by escalating differences of opinion into a brouhaha, a game called "Uproar," or by rejecting all possible solutions and answers with a constant repetition of "Yes But." When Sid did this he was controlling unconsciously and being a difficult person. On the other hand, when he readily agreed with opinions or solutions, as indicated by his silence, he was also frequently difficult, saying later that he really didn't agree in the first place but just "went along." At least when he played "Games," he was not fully aware of what he was doing or why he was doing it. At other times, he was controlling or docile because that was the way he had learned to deal with others "successfully." Ultimately, Sid was a very controlling person, using even his passivity to influence others. Because he couldn't or wouldn't level with others, they found him difficult.

Another example of a difficult person is Ben. Ben, an executive, has good interpersonal relations on the levels of inclusion and control. He tends to include lots of people in his life and he is almost always ready to be included in the lives of others; in fact, he calls himself gregarious. He levels with others in areas of control, in the sense that both he and they know he likes to influence others and does so often. Ben's problems arise in the area of affect. While he includes many people in his life and he is often included in theirs, he tends to get closer to others than he permits others to get close to him. He is friendly, genuinely concerned about the needs of his friends, ready to help however he can. On the other hand he finds it difficult to accept help or concern from others; he behaves so that most people are kept at "arm's length" when they try to get close to him.

When Sid's son had a drug problem, Ben had gotten very close to the family; he was a good counselor to Sid and Micki, Sid's wife, and even managed to be an accepted advisor to Michael, Sid's son with the problem. It was mostly because of Ben's warm and wise support that Michael accepted the right kind of help and "kicked the habit." During this time, Ben spent a good amount of time at Sid's home, dining there a couple of times a week,. He got very close to the whole family. Yet, when, a year later, Ben was going through the pain of a divorce, he listened to the intended support of Sid and Micki with the greatest reluctance. In fact, Sid and Micki often felt as though they were intruding. Ben never said it, but he behaved in ways that said "I can handle this myself. This isn't your business. I don't like you involved in my personal life." Sid and Micki were sad and they were confused; Ben was a very complex man. He was difficult, stubborn and maybe even macho!

Affect refers to the level at which our behavior says that we get close to people *and* we let them get close to us. We may be quite selective, getting close to a few and allowing a few to get close to us. We may be totally open, behaving in ways that say we get close to many people and many people get close to us. In either case, we are understood and interpersonal conflict in this area is unlikely. People might wish we were more or less open, but in time they often accept us for what we are. Confusion and difficulty arise when we seem to be contradictory: like Ben, involving ourselves closely with others but not allowing them to involve themselves with us. That can make us a difficult person.

For the sake of clarity, a word needs to be said about the difference between inclusion and affect. We may include many people in our lives and behave so that we are included in theirs, but not become close or intimate with many. Or we may include only a few people in our lives and behave so that only a few may include us in theirs and be close and intimate with those few. There is a difference between inclusion and affect, since we can include people and be included by them at low levels of relationship: we associate with them as acquaintances or neighbors or fellow workers without developing relationships of closeness, friendship or intimacy. We shall reflect more on this when we speak of how we use our time and the effect that has on our relationships in Chapter 2.

William C. Schutz is an esteemed psychologist whose credentials include not only his work with the U.S. Navy but also four years as lecturer and research associate at Harvard University. If I can keep up with his career, I think he is presently with Esalen in California. When he says that *inclusion, control* and *affect* are central to the patterns of our interpersonal relationships, I believe his findings. I believe him, not only theoretically, but practically in terms of my own experientially painful life span to the present. My inclusion level has been highly selective, my control has been heavy and my affect level has been meager. I have felt the consequences: few social relationships, anxiety in my presence and limited familial relationships. I guess that is why I write about difficult people—because I sense that I am one of them. But I have made progress.

Progress is the name of our styles of interpersonal relationships; unlike personality preferences, which many psychologists say will stay with us throughout our lifetime, our interpersonal styles are learned and, therefore, can be unlearned. We can change the "successful" patterns of inclusion, control and affect that we may now find to be "unsuccessful." We can even out our inclusion index, so that our behavior signals some sort of equilibrium between our inclusion of others and our willingness to be included. We can level our control, so that people know when and why we are influencing and when and why we are docile. We can stop playing "Games." We can balance our affect, so that our behavior brings others as close to us as we want them to be close to us. In other words, interpersonal conflicts are not as difficult to handle as "personality clashes." We have more control.

SURVIVAL STRATEGIES

1. Keep your expectations of people at a reasonable level, especially when you have gotten to know them a bit. Don't expect "Thelma" to accept invitations readily or "Ben" to accept close emotional support. Let them stay comfortable and adjust your own needs. It is easier to adjust our own needs than to create needs in others.

2. Let the non-controlling person at peace. He or she is probably getting fulfillment in other ways than in the area of control. Generally, such people have no interest in controlling others or in being controlled by others.

3. A truly strong "controller" may have to be left alone. This may mean leaving a job where we have such a boss, but that is better than becoming enslaved and crushed.

4. *Sometimes* confrontation can be effective with controllers, provided we "know our person" and the consequences are such that we can handle. Controllers understand confrontation and they can respect its use. But we should have solid ground for believing we can do it effectively before we try. One way to test is with light humor, testing to determine whether the potential confrontee can laugh at himself or herself at all.

5. Low affect people need to know that it's O.K. to be low affect. We do not expect lots of support or compliments from them.

6. High affect people also need to know it's O.K. to be warm and supportive. Don't misinterpret their support as an invitation to intimacy or love, since that will often create serious difficulty for you and for them. Appreciate the fun of having them around, but don't feel you must behave at their level if you really are not a high affect person. That could be exhausting.

7. All of these strategies presume that the other person is content with his or her learned patterns of interpersonal relationships. If such people are not, if they want to change and ask you to help, it's OK to be supportive of their change if you feel your relationship is strong enough to survive such

an effort. Usually, however, friends are not the best people to help friends change. After all, we became friends because we liked each other as we were. A "helper at a distance" may be a better choice to help us change.

Summary

Differences create difficulties because they scare us: we like to deal with the unfamiliar only when we understand it. If we do understand it, there is a chance we may tolerate and even appreciate it. If we are to learn to live with and to work with difficult people, understanding is a first step. Differences are an enrichment, not a problem.

Certainly there are personality differences that trigger clashes. Introverts and extraverts clash because extraverts move too quickly for introverts and introverts are mysterious to extraverts. Intuitives find sensing people pessimistic or plodding, while the sensing perceive intuitives as dreamers or malcontents. Feelers see thinkers as insensitive and thinkers evaluate feelers as unreasonable. Perceivers look on judgers as robots and judgers label perceivers as lazy and disorganized. The fact that each of us generally is either an introvert *or* extravert, an intuitive *or* a sensing person, a feeler *or* a thinker, and a perceiver *or* a judger, gives us a great deal of room for conflict, a large area in which we may be a "difficult person."

The area is broadened further when we realize that interpersonal relationship patterns are learned and added to personality traits. Regardless of our basic personality, we develop ways of dealing with others from childhood through school life. William Schutz has indicated that the most important interpersonal styles encompass *inclusion:* the level at which we include others in our lives *and* behave so as to be included in theirs, *control:* the level at which we behave influentially *and* behave docilely, and *affect:* the level at which we tend to get close to others *and* allow them to get close to us. An imbalance in inclusion or affect, so that our behavior invites more than we accept, or accepts more than we invite, can confuse and create difficulty; an imbalance in control can make us so unpredictable that we need friends to explain us to others.

Personality traits and interpersonal styles are basic to unraveling the mystery of difficult people. Part of the unraveling is understanding and appreciating differences. Traits and styles are usually unconscious, without malice or intent.

"Games" that create difficulties are partially unconscious and unintended, but they are a third layer of behavior that compound difficulties. We need to grasp the dynamics of "Games" if we are to cope with the reality of difficult people.

2

"Games" and Difficulties

Back in 1967 Eric Berne published *Games People Play*. Since I do not write to reinvent the wheel, I will not repeat his book in this chapter, but I do intend to apply some of his thinking to difficult people. Many of us play games, but difficult people play them viciously.

When was the last time you had "bad feelings," but you didn't know why? How often have you had to ask "What happened?" after an encounter, and honestly didn't know the answer? When was the last time you asked yourself "Why did I do that?" and felt the answer too complicated to pursue? What was your most recent "bad feeling"? Were you able to determine its cause? Do you pursue recognition by creating waves, by making mistakes that make others pay attention to you? Do you know those who do, even though you do not? Do you find yourself persecuting subordinates, or behaving so that they persecute you? Do you work with people who seek out your advice, and then blame you if things go wrong? Do you seek out advice and blame others if things go wrong? Do you regularly try to be helpful, only to find that others turn on you and find fault?

If any of these questions "ring bells" for you, this is a chapter you should read. "Games" are verbal exercises that impact the whole person: they are verbal in the sense that they are played with words. The words are clear and call for an expected response from another, but they have hidden meaning and are directed to elicit a particular response from another. The words may be exchanged for an extended amount of time or they may be brief. They always lead to bad feelings on the part

31

of yourself and others. At the moment, the bad feelings are felt but not explained. You and your partner leave in confusion.

Two friends of mine recently played a "Game." Jerry, a born journalist and talented writer, accepted a new job with a book publisher. Mimi has long been his friend. Their conversation went like this:

> **Jerry:** I really liked my job till today. It was a real bummer.
> **Mimi:** Why? What happened?
> **Jerry:** Eric, our editor, asked me to review one of the manuscripts I had recommended. He felt I was too hard on the writer. He suggested that the thing had some potential. But I had given the guy all the benefits I could. I know what I'm doing!
> **Mimi:** You recommended it? That means you thought it had a good deal of potential. What was Eric's gripe?
> **Jerry:** He thought I had asked for too much rewrite.
> **Mimi:** Had you?
> **Jerry:** I don't think so. The parts I suggested for rewrite really needed it. They were not of the same quality as the rest of the work. I respect Eric, though, and I don't know what to do.
> **Mimi:** Could you go over those sections piece by piece with Eric and show him the differences?
> **Jerry:** *Yes, but* I don't think it would do any good. I'm new in the firm, as you know.
> **Mimi:** How about doing some rewriting yourself, then share the differences with Eric?
> **Jerry:** *Yes, but* he might think I'm only blowing my own horn. I'm not sure that Eric respects my judgment sufficiently yet.
> **Mimi:** Then why not contact the author directly and talk over your suggestions with him?
> **Jerry:** *Yes, but* he's been published by us before and he doesn't know me. I'm not sure that would have any effect. He might just run to Eric.

Mimi: If he does, you could question the professional quality of the company; you're only doing your job, right?

Jerry: *Yes, but* it looks as though I'm trying to make my mark at the expense of a proven author.

Mimi: Then, what do you think you should do?

Jerry: God, I don't know. Suppose this is what the job is all about—just pleasing the editor and his pets.

Jerry and Mimi parted that evening, both feeling bad. Without fully intending it, Jerry was out to prove that Mimi couldn't help him. Mimi was "sucked in" to helping because she liked to help. They had played a game. The "Game" is called "Yes, but." Difficult people regularly plan "Games," and they regularly make us feel bad.

Bad feelings (feeling badly) are the objectives of "Games." They are played to avoid intimacy, to avoid responsibility, to make people predictable or to prove our presumptions about ourselves or others. Jerry played "Yes, but" to prove his assumption that Mimi was incompetent to help and to prove that he could not be responsible for his job; no one could, except a "yes" man. He also played so that Mimi would be concerned about him. Our motives for "Games" are multiple. If Jerry were a truly difficult person he would have played the game to the hilt, accusing Mimi of being stupid or insensitive, attacking her genuine concern for him and concluding that she was "no damn good." After Mimi's response of "Then, what do you think you should do?" Jerry would have continued: "What do you think I came to you for? To ask me questions that are obvious? Don't you ever have an original idea? I should have known better than to ask you. God, don't I have any friends with brains? I won't make the mistake of asking your help again." A difficult person leaves you devastated; he or she is vicious, sometimes without intending to be so. And sometimes the more such people hurt, the more vicious they are. Viciousness can be a cry for help—but not always.

"Games" are made up of five components: (1) an overt or surface message, (2) a covert or hidden message, (3) a response or responses from another, (4) all involved feel badly, and (5) the "Game" is played outside of our full awareness. *There is an overt or surface message* we receive. It is what the words say: I'd like your advice; help me; let me help you; what do you mean? The surface message is what is understood by anyone hearing the words. The words can be the same as those used when not playing a "Game"; that is what makes "Games" difficult to spot.

There is a covert message. Something is written between the lines. We may recognize this message readily, if we know the "Gameplayer"; we may have been trapped before by someone who asked for our help; this same someone may approach us again. In Mimi's case, she should recognize Jerry's covert message if he should approach her again: "I know you can't help and I'm going to prove it." "You have nothing to offer I haven't already thought of." The covert or hidden message may not be recognizable until the other has responded once or twice. In the "Yes, but" game a couple of "Yes, but's" with no true reflection on the suggestion is sufficient hint that you are being involved in a "Game." Other "Games," as we shall see, are not so easily recognized.

There is a response. At this point we get "hooked," in the sense that the "Gameplayer" has found a soft spot, an inclination or habit of ours, and has "hooked" us like a fish. We may regularly feel inclined to "help" others, to "give advice," to "be perfect," so that we "know how" to react on every occasion; we may pride ourselves on being "good listeners" or "wise." We can have any number of presumptions about ourselves that predispose us to respond to the "Gameplayer." Once we make a response we are usually in the "Game" for keeps, but, as we shall see, the usual is not necessary; we can stop the "Game" before bad feelings result. If we are very perceptive, and especially if we know the person as a "Gameplayer," we stop the "Game" by not responding as expected. We can refuse to play.

Bad feelings always result from "Games." Some bad feelings are legitimate—when a loved one is lost, a prize possession is stolen or lost, or we grieve over our treatment of another. Genuine bad feelings can be traced back to their source with clarity. The bad feelings that result from "Games" are not so clearly identified in their source; we know we feel bad, but are not quite sure why. We feel confused and disoriented; we only know that we don't feel good about the experience. This is due to our unawareness of "Games."

"Games" are played without full awareness of what is happening. Each of us has hidden parts of our personality, segments that we frequently know little about—the ideas instilled in us by parents or parent figures, the remnants of childish thinking that we have never discarded; they motivate our behavior and influence our thinking without our full realization. Eric Berne called them the Parent and the Child within us. They are not simple memories of our parents and their teachings or of our childhood fairy tales; they are so real and dynamic that when they take over our personality we *are* our parent or we *are* a little boy or girl of four or five. Descriptively, we become another person, and what we do is not fully in our grown-up awareness. Yet, it is our grown-up awareness that is able to recognize and stop "Gameplaying."

Let's repeat Jerry's and Mimi's conversation in the light of these five components. The covert message, outside of full awareness, is in parentheses.

Jerry: I really liked my job till today. It was a real bummer. (CHILD: I need help!)

Mimi: Why? What happened? (PARENT: Ah! How can I help?)

Jerry: Eric, our editor, asked me to review one of the manuscripts I had recommended. He felt I was too hard on the writer. He suggested that the thing had some potential. But I had given the guy all the benefits I could. I know what I'm doing! (CHILD: He did this terrible thing to me. I did my best. I feel bad.)

Mimi: You recommended it? That means you thought it had a good deal of potential. What was Eric's gripe? (PARENT: I'm on your side. Eric doesn't seem to make sense.)

Jerry: He thought I had asked for too much rewrite. (CHILD: He made this stupid request of me!)

Mimi: Had you? (PARENT: Now that we rethink it, did you ask for too much?)

Jerry: I don't think so. The parts I suggested for rewrite really needed it. They were not of the same quality as the rest of the work. I respect Eric, though, and I don't know what to do. (CHILD: I know I'm right, but I don't know what to do.)

Mimi: Could you go over those sections piece by piece with Eric and show him the differences? (PARENT: How about this as a solution?)

Jerry: *Yes, but* I don't think it would do any good. I'm new in the firm, as you know. (CHILD: Gosh, yes, but I'm not respected.)

Mimi: How about doing some rewriting yourself, then share the differences with Eric? (PARENT: O.K., then how about this solution?)

Jerry: *Yes, but* he might think I'm blowing my own horn. I'm not sure that Eric respects my judgment sufficiently yet. (CHILD: Golly, I couldn't do that, ever!)

Mimi: Then why not contact the author directly and talk over your suggestions with him? (PARENT: Maybe if you talked to the person directly . . .)

Jerry: *Yes, but* he's been published before by us and he doesn't know me. I'm not sure that would have any effect. He might just run to Eric. (CHILD: Why would he listen to me? He's got Eric!)

Mimi: If he does, you could question the professional quality of the company; you're only doing your job, right? (PARENT: Jerry, you're a professional; are you sure your colleagues are?)

Jerry: *Yes, but* it looks as though I'm trying to make my mark at the expense of a proven author. (CHILD: I know I'm good, but these guys might cream me!)

Mimi: Then, what do you think you should do? (PARENT: You know best.)

Jerry: God, I don't know. Suppose this is what the job is all about—just pleasing the editor and his pets. (CHILD: I know you can't help. Isn't this a mess?)

If Jerry were truly a difficult person he would have continued with: "What do you think I came to you for? To ask me questions that are obvious? Don't you ever have an original idea? I should have known better than to ask you. God, don't I have any friends with brains? I won't make the mistake of asking your help again." Then Jerry's CHILD would have been in full blossom. All of us play "Games," but difficult people go out of their way to make us feel miserable. If Jerry did not go into full CHILD, both of us would still have felt bad; difficult people have a way of using "Games" to make everyone feel terrible.

Mimi was caught in the "Game" when she responded: "What was Eric's gripe?" She was fully hooked after the second "Yes, but" of Jerry, when she said "Then why not contact the author ..." At that point, after two "Yes, but's" with no consideration given to her suggestions, she should have recognized a "Game." Mimi is "caught" by difficult people because she is so often in her PARENT, too ready to rescue others, offer advice, feel superior in her wisdom or judge others. Mimi is a prime candidate for the difficult person. She becomes difficult to others when they "catch" her without answers they never intended to get.

"Games" are confusing because they are not played with full awareness. Jerry was not consciously trying to "get" Mimi, nor was Mimi consciously trying to be "gotten." Both, in their PARENT or CHILD, thought they were communicating sincerely. Their ADULT was not in gear; the ADULT is that part of our personality that is meant to be the executor of our reactions and interactions, intended to control the PARENT and the CHILD. The PARENT knows what it is doing, but acts only according to the dictates of what we have learned from our parents or parent figures and have accepted without consideration or evaluation. The CHILD knows what it is doing, but only in terms of the limited horizons of childhood. PARENT and CHILD reactions that have not been screened through our ADULT are semi-conscious: they happen without thinking, much as the automatic nervous system (central) keeps our heart beating and our lungs breathing without our conscious awareness.

"Bad feelings" that we do not quite understand tell us that we have been involved in a "Game." Another clue that "Gameplaying" time is here is the switching of roles. Jerry started out to be a VICTIM: "Today was a real bummer!" Mimi started out to be a RESCUER: "Why? What happened?" As the dialogue continued Jerry changed his role to PERSECUTOR: "I won't make the mistake of asking your help again!" Mimi found her role changed to VICTIM. Stephen Karpman suggested these three roles of *Persecutor, Rescuer* and *Victim* to be visible in "Gameplaying"; the shift from one role to another, he theorized, indicates the presence of a "Game."

Ann, a secretary in Accounting, approaches Vicky, a business friend who is in Purchasing:

Ann: Vicky, I need some advice. Would you help me? (VICTIM)

Vicky: Sure, Ann, what can I do for you? (RESCUER)

Ann: I need somebody to help me decide what to do. I got a bad performance appraisal yesterday and I really am not getting along with my boss. He thinks I'm not loyal to Accounting, that I have no enthusiasm for my job.

Vicky: Oh.

Ann: Vicky, there's this great job opening up over at Grams, our competitor; I really am tired of working in the lousy atmosphere in Accounting here. But I can't decide whether to apply for the job at Grams or not. If my boss found out and I didn't get the Grams job, my life would be even more miserable here. What do you think?

Vicky: If I were in your shoes, I'd sure apply, honey. From what you've told me, things can't get much worse. And you have a chance to move ahead at Grams.

Ann applied, did not get the job and her boss found out. The following took place a week or so after the conversation described above.

Vicky: How are things going, Ann?
Ann: Vicky, would you butt out of my life? If it weren't for you, I'd be a lot happier right now! (PERSECUTOR)
Vicky: Oh, I'm sorry. What did I do? (VICTIM)
Ann: You know damn well what you did—you and your lousy advice! (PERSECUTOR)

Ann walked away feeling badly; Vicky sat down, also feeling badly. Neither was very clear on what had happened. A "Game" had come to its predictable conclusion. The problem was that neither Ann or Vicky was fully aware that each was heading to such a conclusion. Vicky thought she was helping; Ann found someone to blame. Vicky had played from her PARENT and Ann from her CHILD. After a week or so, they switched roles: Vicky from *Rescuer* to *Victim* and Ann from *Victim* to *Persecutor*. Vicky moved into her CHILD and Ann into her PARENT.

Why "Gameplaying"?

"Gameplaying" is so frequent and universal that the question of why we play "Games" is not often asked; we don't ask questions about seemingly normal behavior. If we do wonder why he or she or I might behave this way or that, our answer is usually, "That's the way he or she is or I am." But the question needs to be asked when we are trying to cope with or to live with difficult people. Understanding is the taproot of tranquillity.

We play "Games" to get attention, to get noticed. "Games" give us negative attention, most of the time, but even that is better than being ignored. They also give us positive attention, compliments, as they progress, but the end result is always negative. Jerry got Mimi's attention by sharing his concerns with her; Mimi felt good that Jerry would confide in her. Ann made Vicky notice her when she asked for advice and Vicky was complimented that Ann thought enough of her to ask her advice. In the end both Jerry and Ann aroused attention with their difficult response, and Mimi and Vicky received the attention of the attack.

All of us need attention, a kind of psychological cuddling that grows out of our need for physical cuddling as infants and children. Infants die without such human interaction; we grown-ups die psychologically without human interaction at the level of being noticed, for good or for ill. Anything is better than being ignored, so if we cannot get compliments, we play "Games" to get invectives.

Another reason we play "Games" is to avoid intimacy: a CHILD to CHILD relationship that allows us to be totally open with each other. Intimacy is not necessarily sexual; it is a closeness that involves vulnerability; genuine friendship means being vulnerable to another, a willingness to be hurt by another because we are sharing with the other all that we have: ourselves. If we are afraid of intimacy, we might play "Games." In intimacy we share our innermost selves with another; if they reject that, we have nothing more to offer; we are rejected without hope of recapitulation. It is the end! "Games" help us to avoid such finality. "Games" permit us to say: "But this is what I meant; I didn't mean that! I'm surprised you took it that way. I'm disappointed in you." "Games" give us the excuse of not leveling; we try to manipulate, because we cannot but keep the "other" at arm's-length. Only then can we feel safe and in control.

"Games" allow us to avoid responsibility. Jerry could say: "I've got no one to help me. No wonder I can't get anywhere!" Ann could say: "My life is all your fault, Vicky." Difficult people like to place blame on others. They do not like to accept responsibility for their own actions.

Difficult people like to be in control; they like to predict the result of human interaction; risks are disconcerting. "Games" make people predictable, even though we play them without realizing our goal. "Games" make people safe. There are no surprises. In our unconscious, we know where we are going, while the other person may not. Others become VIC-

TIMS, at least for the time being. In human discourse, the end result of a discussion, a conversation or interaction is unknown. "Gameplaying" eliminates this risk. There is always a "predictable payoff" or conclusion when we play a "Game," and difficult people play in order to avoid surprises. Again, they like to be in control.

Difficult people also play "Games" to prove their own convictions about themselves or about others. The "Games" we have seen with Jerry and Mimi and Ann and Vicky illustrate this dynamic. Jerry was convinced that Mimi really couldn't help him, although he was not thinking this consciously. So, he played *"Yes, but"* with Mimi; he did not intend to accept her help from the very beginning. Ann intended to prove that Vicky wasn't really competent to help her, and, in fact, would hurt her; so she played the "If It Weren't for You" game with Vicky, shifting all responsibility for her sorrowful position on Vicky. Jerry's conviction about himself was: "I have to go it alone, even if I can't make it," and Ann's conviction was: "I can't make it and neither could anyone else in my position!" Both Jerry and Ann played a "Game" to reinforce their views of themselves. Without "Games" they might find that they are not what they think they are. But that would be hard to handle. So, they remain difficult people and try to make others difficult.

These are some reasons why people play "Games"; there are others, but these are the most obvious reasons. "Why" people play "Games" is important. More important is how do we avoid being hooked by "Games." How do we manage to work with and live with such difficult people without becoming a part of their vicious world?

Avoiding "Games"

The best way to avoid "Games" is to keep the ADULT in us in charge of the situation. This means that our PARENT or CHILD does not go off on its own, leaving our ADULT awareness in the dark. Each of us can recognize the PARENT in action: the nurturing "Ahh," the cooing "Let me help," the pointed finger in the face of another, the concerned tone, the harsh scold, etc. PARENT includes all of the words, actions, tones we learned from our parents or parent figures, all of the kinds of things we associate with parents today. Most of our PARENT messages are good and necessary; the examples given above can all be appropriate in the right situation. To avoid "Games" the ADULT needs to play a part in determining what PARENT activity is appropriate and when it is appropriate.

Mimi, in the example of Jerry and Mimi, could have short-circuited the "Game" after the second of Jerry's *Yes, buts* by stating from her ADULT: "Jerry, you haven't taken time to consider the two alternatives I've already given you. Maybe we could talk again after you've given them some thought; or maybe we could talk about their pro's and con's here and now." Vicky, if she had sensed a "Game" in progress with Ann, could have replied from her ADULT to Ann's request for advice: "Certainly I'll help, but I'm not going to tell you what to do. What are some possibilities you've already thought about?" Vicky could have appropriately used her PARENT to be supportive of Ann but not to make decisions for her. We cannot always avoid getting involved in a "Game," but we can often stop the "Game" by shifting to our ADULT and encouraging the other person to do the same, that is, to move from his or her PARENT or CHILD to his or her ADULT. We need not even mention that we sense a "Game," since this might trigger another "Game" in which shouting louder leads to bad feelings; people often feel accused when told they are "playing a Game," and, consequently, become defensive so that they can attain the goal of bad feelings! Avoid jargon; just make the right shift to sidetrack the suspected "Game."

Keeping in mind Stephen B. Karpman's theory of "Games," we can stop their progress by not *playing* PERSECUTOR, VICTIM or RESCUER. Remember, Karpman sees these as *roles*; we assume the role to attain the payoff of bad feelings or because we have been caught up in a "Game." Certainly there are times when we need to persecute, to accept the fact that we are a victim or to rescue another in genuine need. Karpman is not speaking of these real needs. The "Game" PERSECUTOR, VICTIM or RESCUER assumes the role when there is no real need for such a function. Jerry was not really a VICTIM, nor did he need a RESCUER, the role taken by Mimi. He could have benefited by talking out his problem with someone he respected, but this dialogue would have looked quite different from the one that is described above. The conversation might have gone like this:

Jerry: Mimi, I really like my job, but I ran into a problem today that I'd like to share with you and get your reactions. (ADULT directing CHILD)

Mimi: I'd be glad to help if I can. Why don't you tell me about it. (ADULT directing PARENT)

Jerry would then describe the situation to Mimi and Mimi might try to help him clarify some points with appropriate questions. Together they could explore possible solutions, leaving Jerry to make any final decisions.

In other words, we can avoid or stop "Games" by not taking on roles that are not needed or indicated as real in this particular situation.

Closely allied to refusing to take on unnecessary roles is a third approach to avoiding "Games." DO NOT EXAGGERATE the strengths or weaknesses of ourselves or of others. Ann exaggerated Vicky's strength as an advisor and her own weakness in decision making. Ann could have seen Vicky as a knowledgeable friend and "sounding board," and probably would have approached her much differently. She might have asked Vicky to help her think out a decision she had to make, but she need not rely upon Vicky as priestess and director. Ann might have been more realistic about her own power to make her own decisions and her strength to take responsibility for them. The same dynamic could operate between Jerry and Mimi, were they not given to exaggeration.

SURVIVAL STRATEGIES

1. Learn to recognize "Games" so you can avoid them.

   a. Know yourself well enough to recognize what "hooks" you: helping others (even if help is not needed)? conflict? belittling others? belittling yourself? Watch for the hook that is after your soft spot.
   b. Watch for the telltale signs of "Games": the whining "Would you help me?", the second "Yes, but" with no discussion of previous suggestions, the aggressive remark that invites you to fight.

2. *Think* before you respond. The Adult is our thinking machine and never plays "Games."
3. Even when you recognize the invitation to a "Game," don't accuse others of playing them. This generally leads to "Gameplaying" of one kind or another. Rather, respond from your Adult.
4. Don't take on the *roles* of victim, rescuer or persecutor. There are real victims, rescuers and persecutors, but not in "Games." Remember, "Games" are *played*. They are *pretend*.
5. Don't exaggerate the weaknesses or strengths of yourself or of others. Recognize your own worth and the worth of others. Recognize your own needs and the needs of others.
6. Don't respond as expected if you suspect a "Game." Don't give a "kick" from your Parent if that is what is expected; make a humorous remark with your Child. Don't crumble into your Child before a persecuting remark; respond with your Adult.
7. Don't be disappointed when you find yourself in a "Game." We all get trapped once in a while. If you can recognize it, you will at least know why you are feeling bad!

Summary

There are lots of "Games" that create difficulties and that are used by difficult people. In this chapter we have detailed the games of "Yes, but" and "IWFY" ("If It Weren't for You"). The dynamics of all "Games" are the same: an opener that hooks some interest deeply rooted in us; we respond only to find that the "tables are turned" and things are happening we never expected; we are confused and feel badly, for reasons that are not quite clear.

Briefly, some "Games" that difficult people play are:

"Now I've Got You, You Son of a Bitch" (NIGYSOB): help is offered from the PARENT; the VICTIM takes the offer seriously only to find that when he or she asks for it, he or she is PERSECUTED:

Boss: This is an excellent report you assembled. Your secretaries did a fine job, but in the future don't feel you have to do everything yourself. Come to me when you need help.

Me: I really appreciate that offer. As a matter of fact, I am in a bind on the follow-up survey. Could some of your people help me with it?

Boss: I like to think we all pull our weight around here. We are busy enough in our area without taking on your work as well!

"Kick Me": behavior is such that it begs to be noticed with a put-down:

Boss: That was a fine piece of work you did on the road last week.

Me: Thank you, but I think I could have accomplished a lot more.

Boss: Why? What do you mean?

Me: Well, I could have covered a lot more territory if I had pushed a bit.

Boss: I didn't realize that. But it's probably true. I truly think you could have done a lot more, now that you point it out! I've always suspected you were holding out on us. From now on, work to your full potential; I'll be keeping an eye on you from now on.

For a complete discussion of "Games" that create difficulties for all of us and are used with dexterity by difficult people see *Games People Play* by Eric Berne, M.D. (Grove Press, N.Y., 1967). This chapter has offered a bird's-eye view of one of the ways difficult people make life difficult for us. "Games" consist of a series of human exchanges that have hidden meanings and always lead to bad feelings. They are played without full awareness, almost out of habits that have been found successful in the past. Many of us play "Games," but they seem to be a particularly favorite form of human interaction among difficult people.

Sometimes we can avoid "Games" or at least stop their progress once they are suspected. Best of all, we can shift to an ADULT response and help the "Gameplayer" to do the same. We can also recognize that we have taken on a role that is not realistic and refuse to *play Persecutor, Victim* or *Rescuer.* We can save those functions for times when they are genuine and needed. We can also take care not to exaggerate our own or others' strengths or weaknesses; exaggerations in these areas often set the stage for a "Game."

We have discussed some of the reasons people play "Games." One final caution: "Games" are so necessary to some people that even more serious problems can arise when they are deprived of them. If we play "Games" to gain recognition, we need to learn how to get recognition without "Gameplaying." It can be dangerous to deprive another of his or her "Game" unless we have something to offer to take its place. We need to be supportive, to notice, to give other attention in healthy ways, if we are going to take away another's "Games." Such supplementation may not always be our responsibility, but sometimes it is. When we choose to change the behavior of another, we sometimes assume significant responsibilities for the other.

Certainly, we do not assume such responsibility when we try only to avoid being trapped into "Games" ourselves or when we choose to stop a "Game" in progress. That is what we are usually trying to do when we cope or strive to work with difficult people.

3

Difficult People "One On One"

We make assumptions about people every day, often based on pre-conceived notions of physical appearance, speech patterns or first impressions. Youth, hair length or dress may help or hinder our hearing of another, depending on our assumptions. Sometimes we are on target: first impressions, for instance, are worth listening to.

We also have assumptions about ourselves, convictions, often unspoken and only dimly in our consciousness, about how we are to behave and how well we can expect to succeed. They have been planted in our psyche when we were most vulnerable, probably between the ages of five and seven. During that period we were desperate in our effort to identify who we were and what was expected of us; any tidbit of information was acceptable. If we were told "Don't cry" often enough we may have interpreted this to mean that we were not to acknowledge our feelings; if we were told "you wouldn't understand" often enough, we could have understood that to mean that we were supposed to be stupid; if we were told to be "perfect," we might still be feeling frustrated that we have not reached that goal. These and other early assumptions about ourselves can contribute to the difficulty we find with people "one-on-one." Others are not always the sole source of difficulty.

Difficulty can be a value. It is not always negative. Difficulty can be perceived as an enrichment, an added motivation and a source of cohesion; if it is, then difficult people can be a source of enriching stimulation and deepening relationships. Of course, difficulty can also be destructive. The point of this chapter is that it need not always be destructive! Sometimes, perhaps more frequently than we think, it can be life-giving. When we find difficulty "one-on-one" we need to look for the life-giving advantage that makes coping worth our while.

Difficulties can make the energy available for our work even greater. We are forced to look at perspectives and facets we may not have considered, or considered only superficially. We may now be forced to review new dimensions in some depth. Also, we may find new motivation, be forced to look at realities we would not previously consider. We may be pushed to new levels of creativity and innovation, reflecting on ideas and conceptions we previously left untouched or slightly considered. In the end, we may find solutions or ideas that promise to be more effective than those we had come upon before the difficulty.

The fact is that where there are few or no difficulties, differences in perception, opinion or direction, productivity is usually low. We tend to talk to ourselves, concluding, of course, that we are correct! Still, differences have to be managed. Without management, they tend to restrict information, create additional difficulties and distort information even further. The key to management is recognition, acknowledgment of difficulties and the differences that contribute to them.

Difficulties challenge us to discover roots, sources and reasons, all of which will surface later if they are not managed now. No doubt, we would like to live and work without difficulties, but that is not likely in this world. The philosopher Leibniz said that we live in the best of possible worlds; if we do, then the best of possible worlds includes difficulties and differences. We need to recognize their source if we are to have them serve our needs.

Assumptions about Others

We can create difficulties in many ways, one of which is to make assumptions about others. Usually, our behavior indicates our assumptions.

My Uncle Ed had a moon face! I don't know how he made

his living, since I knew him only as a man we visited rarely when I was a small child. But he seemed cold and indifferent. He was bald. As a child, I reacted to Uncle Ed: I didn't like people who were moon-faced and bald! I didn't like cold people!

Unfortunately, men with those facial images are still a problem to me. I find it difficult to take seriously a man with a moon face and bald head. I "write them off." This is probably my misfortune, since not all "moon-faced-bald" individuals deserve to be "written-off."

Physical characteristics can present us with difficulties. Long hair can turn us "off" in a man; heavy make-up can turn us "off" with a woman. Short skirts, a plunging neckline, fluttering eyebrows can trigger assumptions that may or may not be valid. Tight pants, staring and a ruddy complexion may also tell us things that are not true. Much depends upon our reading and experience of the past. The issue is that we do make assumptions upon the physical characteristics of others. They determine, to some extent, our reactions to another—and, *sometimes,* those reactions are valid.

We tend to react to the dress of another. The woman who wears a suit may call forth a kind of behavior the woman in the dress does not; the boss who always has a "pocket handkerchief" can demand reactions that the boss in a jacket cannot; slacks worn by a secretary elicit a different response than a dress worn by the same secretary. How we dress often indicates how we expect to be treated! Our clothes build on our assumptions about others. They also say something about our expectations of ourselves.

Whole careers have been built on the expertise of "knowing how to dress." The underlying assumption is that our physical image speaks to others, influences their decisions so that perceptions favor us; we are at the mercy of others' perceptions. And they are at our mercy.

From this perspective, our assumptions about others can *create* difficult people where there are none. Influenced by our own "convictions," reinforced by the "perceptions" of others, we may well make decisions, decisions that manufacture problems where there are none. This is the problem with assumptions about others.

But how about first impressions? They are made by facial presentations, expressions and by dress. Contrary to the wisdom of folklore, they should not be ignored. Each of us has a simple, innocent, natural child part of our personality, and it is dependable. It is this child part of the personality that makes an evaluation of an individual when first we meet him or her. The child may not be accurate entirely, but it deserves attention. It has the power to "pick up" on clues that we otherwise might miss: the smile, the flit of the eye or the shrug of the shoulder. First impressions are not infallible, but they do see things that later involvement tends to blot out.

As an experiment, reflect back on your first impressions about someone with whom you are having difficulties. Think about that first meeting. See what you find.

Assumptions about others are first found in ourselves, our upbringing, our training, our experience. Today, when emphasis is placed upon the facade, the appearance of another, those assumptions can be reinforced: impressions may be accurate or faulty, reactions to the real person or to a facade. Unless we take the trouble to discover the difference, we may find difficulty. Impressions, even first impressions, and assumptions can be accurate; they can also be seriously faulty. We may trust the untrustworthy or mistrust the dependable.

It is impossible not to make assumptions about others. It is unwise not to examine those assumptions.

Assumptions about Ourselves

Our assumptions about others are almost always influenced by our assumptions about ourselves. Assumptions, after all, involve a relationship of some kind, whether they are made from a distance or from closeness, and relationships involve myself and another. I can make an assumption only about another from my own perspective. My own perspective is often colored by my assumptions about myself.

George, a senior accountant, is a *perfectionist*. He is good at his job, able to track down an errant penny through the underbrush of corporate trillions. His most trying experience has been coping with fellow workers with sloppy desks; he has no children. Departmental decision making, organized to allow the contributions of all employees, is a nightmare to George, simply because he *knows* that the best decision is unlikely to be made. Compromise will be the outcome.

A few weeks ago George worked with Josie, a public relations consultant, on preparing a presentation for a stockholders' meeting. Josie aimed at making the presentation brief, understandable and attractive. George agonized over the gaps and simplifications of the presentation; it was simply not accurate or complete. The presentation was not perfect; it was truncated! Josie found George difficult. George found Josie difficult.

George assumes that he must be perfect; as a result, he finds patience elusive, works as hard on trivial detail as he does on major issues and produces little of lasting value because his efforts rarely meet his expectations of perfection. George finds life with others difficult. Probably George was told when he was growing up that he was to be perfect; four out of five "A's" on his report card were never noticed, but the one "B" was singled out: "What happened there, son?" His expectations of himself were reinforced by teachers and fellow students, who expressed surprise if George did not excel. He carried these expectations of perfection into business and now creates a good deal of stress for himself and for others.

Bertha carries about different assumptions about herself. She does not expect perfection. She assumes that *no matter how hard she tries, she will not succeed.* She remembers being told frequently: "Success is not everything," "Well, at least you tried, honey," and even "Girl, you have two strikes against you already: you're a girl and you're black!" Bertha assumes that she isn't going to "make it."

Her assumptions about herself have probably contributed to Bertha's earnest efforts that never quite succeed. For five years she has been a clerk typist; bosses seem to take her work for granted. She has never been nominated for management training; in fact, she has applied for several secretarial positions only to be rejected. She sees herself trying very hard, but is not quite able to say: "I will *do* it!" She always says: "I'll *try*."

Bertha's difficulties come from her own disappointment and poor self-image. Occasionally she gets depressed and takes out her anger on her peers or family members. Only dimly does she understand that she is her own worst enemy, regularly convincing herself that she will not succeed no matter how hard she tries. Her assumption, of course, shows up in her behavior: shoulders slump, a whine is detectable in her tone of voice and she usually does not look others in the eye. She gives the impression of someone "trying very hard." Others may find her difficult because she is depressing. There is little "joy of life."

Bill and Charlie, on the other hand, seem to be filled with the "joy of life." They tackle everything as though it should have been done last week. They are the *speed kings* of the organization. Some of this frenetic behavior may be attributed to the pace required in the organization, but Bill and Charlie do everything in a hurry. Some say they even make love in a hurry.

Bill and Charlie are driven—driven by their assumption about themselves that they must always "hurry up." It is likely that parents or teachers frequently told them they were slow and that they should "hurry up." They were the little boys all of us have seen trailing behind their parents in the park, while the parents shouted to them: "Hurry up." So, now they do. They drum their fingers on tables waiting for another to finish talking, they drive others frantic with their anxiety, they walk fast, talk fast and drive fast. While they enjoy each other's company, those not on the "fast track" find them nerve racking. By many, they are considered difficult people. They succeed, but at great cost to themselves and to others.

Jonathan is an intellectual. He feels no need for speed. He feels no need for success (at least that is what he says). Jonathan feels very little. Once, when asked whether he was angry after a board meeting, he responded: "Yes, I was angry, but that doesn't bother me." Jonathan's assumption about himself is that he is *not to feel.* As a district manager he cannot understand why salesmen expect praise: "They're doing their job. That's all. It's a business arrangement. Don't expect to be mollycoddled. That's not my job." If Jonathan gives a compliment, it is given with a crooked smile that sometimes makes the recipient cringe. But, that doesn't happen often.

Many years ago Jonathan was told: "Little boys don't cry," or "Anger isn't acceptable in this house, son!" He was told often enough so that he got the message: "Feelings are not important." He found life much better when he didn't express feelings, even feelings of tenderness. It was not long before he convinced himself that he didn't feel at all. So, he stopped admitting he felt. Therefore today he could say: "Yes, I was angry, but that doesn't bother me." He truly believes he doesn't feel; he doesn't own his feelings. He sees himself, and others, as a brain on stilts.

Jonathan perceives himself as an ironman, and expects others to be the same; he insults, ignores and belittles others with impunity. He is a difficult person. He sees feelings as weakness. In his loneliness, he decides that others avoid him because his standards are so high; he is so far superior to them that he makes them feel uncomfortable. "Well, that's the way it is," he concludes, and continues on his blind path. Jonathan's assumption about himself makes him a difficult person. The root of his difficulty is that he admits to being half a person and deals with others as half persons.

Ivan, on the other hand, was never satisfied to conclude: "They don't like me. Well, that's the way it is." Ivan *wanted to be liked.* His assumption about himself was that he was *born to please others.* As a salesman, Ivan was well liked. He often went out of his way for a customer, even to the point where he was taken for granted. His time was spent on servicing, rather than on selling. He never was quite successful, but he was appreciated. Ivan was a difficult person to himself. He was difficult to others in the sense that they never felt as though they were dealing with a real person; there was something phony about Ivan, or so others thought. He wasn't real. He was difficult to his boss because Ivan didn't seem to be using his time and contacts well: Ivan was a popular person, but not a salesman.

Probably, Ivan discovered early in life that things were more pleasant when he pleased others: parents, brothers, sisters, teachers, uncles, aunts, etc. He wasn't supposed to satisfy himself; he was supposed to satisfy others. He learned early to "nod his head" in agreement, to smile a lot and to be obedient. His tone of voice was frequently whiny, outstretched hands indicating "whatever you say" came naturally to him, and he learned to put up with a tight stomach. Ivan was difficult for himself, physically and emotionally.

In his way, Ivan was difficult for others. His advice was sought only if the other was looking for someone to agree with him or her. Ivan was not expected to be innovative or challenging to authority; he was dull and uninteresting. Everyone liked him; few took him seriously; fewer risked friendship. Somehow, Ivan was unreal. He was predictable: he would always seek to please.

Adjustments to Difficulties

Many of our assumptions about others and about ourselves are unconscious; the assumptions are real, we are real, others are real, but we are often unaware of the presence or impact of our assumptions upon our relationships. Assumptions are hidden directors of behavior. We adjust to the difficulty, rather than confront it.

All of us, ourselves as well as those with whom we find difficulty, make adjustments to live with frustration, anxiety and conflict. Some of the ways we adjust are the following. We may find ourselves or others in several categories.

We *compensate*. We (myself or another) have not been promoted as expected; years may pass without our hard work being recognized. Yet, we work overtime, devote enormous energy to clubs and organizations having little to do with the way we earn a living. We are trying to make up for our feelings of incompetence; we are trying to prove to others and to ourselves that the company has overlooked a valuable talent.

When we have done this long enough to become worn out, we become *apathetic* and *bored*. We are ready to resign or to remain "on board" as "dead wood."

We *convert*. When we have been rejected by the boss, had a promising project fail or failed to meet a goal of which we were "sure," we develop back pains, headache or a violent mood with subordinates. We convert or *displace* the real cause of frustration, enabling us to focus attention on our own ills or upon the shortcomings of others.

We *fantasize*. We dream of scenarios in which present superiors will have to come to us for direction and help. We keep them waiting outside of our office for hours. We *take flight* from our job where we have experienced rejection or frustration, either physically, by "having to be on the road," or psychologically, by ignoring the job requirements for a period of time. Probably we have been negatively criticized by the boss, had a favorite proposal rejected or found our authority limited. So, we escape in the "only" way we can.

We *fixate or regress*. We are promoted and find ourselves doing many of the tasks we did before the promotion. A secretary promoted to manager, for instance, continues to make her own copies or does her own typing. Even after some months of succeeding as a manager she finds herself regressing to secretarial behavior if she is frustrated in an administrative effort. She fixates or regresses to where she found success.

We *identify*. To enhance our self-esteem we take on the mannerisms and behavior of another, even internalizing values and norms that are not truly ours. We consciously choose to become "one of the boys" and to sacrifice our own selfhood and individuality. We share the glory and the sorrow of the other, without either having any genuine meaning for us. This is one characteristic of the overly ambitious. It often leads to *repressing* much that is genuine and sincere within us. Sometimes it leads to even greater and more serious frustration than that we sought to avoid by identifying.

We *rationalize*. We (myself or another) justify our errors by pointing to distractions, over-commitment or being understaffed. We say "Everyone does it" or "At the time there was no other way to do it" and walk out on the situation that is still unresolved and filled with confusion. We become *negative* when confronted with the problem we have helped to create: "Do what you want" or "I don't know" makes us resistant passively; "Your people can't handle this job" or "That is contrary to our policy" brings us to active resistance. We may have taken on more than we can handle, received an assignment we didn't want or have found ourselves trapped where we least expected. We try to justify our situation or blame others.

We *project*. Confronted with real or potential conflict we attribute our feelings to others: "they" are the poor decision makers, "they" are ambitious, or "they" don't understand the situation. Sometimes we project because we feel that others are out to "get us." Often we are not in touch with our own feelings and motivations; we are truly unconscious; we don't know what is going on within ourselves. So we disown it and attribute it to others. We will not own our feelings, but we can find them in others.

Strategies for Difficult People

We are not able to eradicate difficulties; they are part of the world in which we live. We can alleviate them by looking at ourselves and by trying to understand others. Handling the difficult self is a twofold task: we need to grow in awareness to ourselves and in awareness to others. Sometimes difficulties are one-sided; sometimes they are more complex. We need to know the difference.

Examine our own assumptions about others and their possible assumptions about others as well as about us. As tidy and businesslike as we think we are, or as others think they are, most of us carry personal assumptions and traits into our worklife. We speak through filters; we hear through filters. Filters take a myriad of forms: "I know what she is going to say," "What does this 'kid' know?" "This guy is after my job." "This is a trap." "I'm not giving in to any louse." Sometimes it is difficult to hear another over the rumblings in our own heads; sometimes it is difficult to hear others because they are not

saying what they mean. In either instance, we are hearing/
talking through filters. We hear what we want to hear or expect to hear; we say what we don't want to say verbally, but
we say it by our tone of voice, our gesture or bodily posture.
Only the astute listener will hear our genuine message, the listener who has learned to bypass filters.

*Our assumptions are sometimes the result of experience,
which may or may not have been a valid experience, that is, it
may or may not have been as we perceived it.* More often assumptions are the progeny of "convictions" implanted in us
by parents, grandparents, aunts, uncles, brothers, sisters,
teachers, etc. The key that unlocks an assumption is the question: "Have we examined it in the light of adult reasoning?" If
we have, and have chosen to adopt it, it is our assumption, for
good or ill; if we have not, it is somebody else's assumption that
we are living by. If it is truly our assumption, it is conscious; if
it is another's, it is unconscious. If it is ours, we can control it; if
it is another's, we cannot control it. Living and hearing
through the assumptions of others is most dangerous because it
restricts our freedom. Unconsciously we disallow ourselves options, the options our assumptions rule out before we even
hear the scenario. If they are our conscious assumptions, we
can always suspend them, because they are in our control.

*Like assumptions, motivations need to be surfaced, to be
made conscious.* Motivations are much more sensitive and personal than assumptions; sometimes we do not know what
makes us do the things we do; we certainly do not know what
motivates others unless they tell us, and even then we might
not know, since it is likely that they are as blind as we are
when it comes to understanding clearly our own motivations.
We err if we ever *presume* to *judge* motivations of another.
Still, we have indicators in major areas that help us to understand what *may* be driving us or others. There are behavioral
hints, but they are *only* hints.

George, described above, is a *perfectionist*, his assumption
being that he had to be perfect and his motivation being perfection. He frequently uses words like "obviously," "clearly,"
"of course," "I think," and "efficacious." His voice tone is often

clipped and righteous, almost pontifical. He counts on his fingers, cocks his wrist and scratches his head; his posture is erect and rigid; his facial expression is stern.

Bertha, profiled above, is a *try hard but never succeed* person. Her favorite words are "It's hard," "I can't," "I'm not sure," and "I don't know." Her tone of voice is impatient, almost challenging help from someone; her fists are often clenched and moving. She sits forward a lot, elbows on her legs; she wears a slight frown or perplexed look.

Bill and Charlie are the *hurrying* people. We spoke of them above. They are always saying things like "We've got to hurry," "I've got to go," and "Well, let's get going." When they speak their voices go up and down frequently; they squirm and tap their fingers; they move quickly, frown and have shifty eyes. Motors are always running, red lights flickering, muscles rippling.

Jonathan, the intellectual described above, is the *strong, non-feeling* person. He is the "brain-on-stilts." His reaction is "no comment" or "I don't care"; his tone is monotone and hard. Jonathan's hands are rigid and arms are often folded, his posture rigid, one leg over the other or wrapped around the other. His facial expression is plastic, unrevealing and uninviting. Jonathan communicates the unimportance of feelings, motivated by the conviction that feelings only complicate matters (which is true, but necessary).

Ivan, also described above, assumes that he must *please everyone* and is regularly motivated to try to do so. His favorite phrases are "you know," "could you," "can you," and "kinda." As a high school teacher he would probably be crushed by Thanksgiving. His voice is often a high whine and his hands seem always to be outstretched. His head nods frequently, agreeing with as much of what he hears as possible, and his eyebrows are often raised, his face looking away from others. If he does not please others, things will not go well, or so he assumes. In fact, things might be much better for himself and for others if he were not blind to his own assumptions and motivations.

Behavior such as this can only be a hint. It is based on the work of Taibi Kahler, Ph.D. and Hedges Capers, Div.M, LHD and comes out of the theory of Transactional Analysis (cf. T. Kahler, H. Capers, "The Miniscript," *Transactional Analysis Journal*, IV:1, January 1974). My purpose in presenting this material here is to give us some strategies to understand our own possible motivations and the motivations of others, with the hope that from understanding will come better ways to work with the difficult self in ourselves and in others.

Even though the descriptions above can give us only a hint of our assumptions and motivations, the categories described are important. To categorize human behavior at all is difficult; the above descriptions are an effort to do that difficult task. The categories are non-exclusive (I'm sure there are many other ways to "file" our behavior and motivations). But they are *one way* to look at ourselves, and one way is better than a lot of description and talk. We need to know or suspect something of our assumptions about ourselves and about others, something about our unconscious motivations, if we are to handle difficulty one-on-one.

We need to ask ourselves some questions and to be able to interpret the responses. That is the purpose of the following instrument. It is not meant to be scientifically structured; it is meant to be thought-provoking, a means of getting a perspective on ourselves and a possible perspective on others.

Exploring Perceptions of Ourselves and of Others

Respond to the following as honestly as you can. No one will know your responses nor your score unless you choose to share them with others. Take your time, but remember, your first response is usually the most accurate. Get to know yourself and others, as you perceive them. You may take this instrument for yourself and/or for another (with whom you might be having difficulty). It is best if you take it first for yourself. To take it for another, simply change the pronouns from "I" to "He" or "She".

Section I:

Register your reactions to the following statements:
1 = I disagree   2 = I somewhat agree   3 = I agree

1. The color of a person is a matter of indifference to me.   _____

2. The age of a person is a matter of indifference to me.   _____

3. My experience with bosses has been good.   _____

4. My co-workers share a lot with me.   _____

5. All minority group members deserve special treatment.   _____

6. Interracial marriage is healthy.   _____

7. Executives care little for the common worker.   _____

8. Bosses are concerned for the common worker.   _____

9. I take older co-workers seriously.   _____

10. I find the enthusiasm of younger people exciting.   _____

11. I feel inferior in my job position.   _____

12. Long hair on a woman is beautiful.   _____

13. Long hair on a man is distasteful.   _____

14. Managers don't do much work.   _____

Analysis: this section helps us to reflect on our assumptions.

1. "I agree" indicates few, if any, assumptions about color. Responses 1 and 2 offer us matter for thought. Why does color make a difference for us? Are we justified in our thinking? Should we be justified?

2. "I somewhat agree" indicates fewer assumptions than the other responses. "I disagree" and "I agree" indicate that we put too little or too much emphasis on age. Age can be a source of wisdom or despair, depending upon who is aged.

3. This response doesn't tell you anything: only what you've experienced. Your experience might be useful or useless, depending upon whether you learned from it or not. The statement is here only to ask you to think about how others have affected your thinking.

4. "I agree" probably indicates that you live with few assumptions. People rarely share a lot with those they see as predictable, with those whose response is foreknown (unless they want that response). A lot of sharing indicates you are seen as quite "open."

5. This calls for an intellectual opinion and the response means little. "I agree" could point to an assumption if you are a minority; "I disagree" could point to an assumption also, if you are not a minority member. Probably "I somewhat agree" indicates fewer assumptions, but it is still an intellectual response. Our assumptions are more emotional and behavioral than intellectual.

6. "I somewhat agree" may indicate few assumptions, since inter-racial marriages are no more or less healthy than other marriages. It depends upon the people.

7. "I somewhat agree" indicates that you are unwilling to group all executives in the same classification; some executives care little for and others are quite concerned for the common worker. Any other response might indicate assumptions worth considering.

8. "I somewhat agree" indicates fewer assumptions. The reasoning is the same made for question number 7.

9. "I somewhat agree" indicates that you realize that age or seniority does not automatically demand serious attention;

it depends upon the person. Other responses might indicate assumptions worth considering.

10. Your response probably depends upon the young people of whom you are thinking, but "I disagree" or "I agree" might indicate an assumption against or for young people that may cause difficulties.

11. Unless you are just learning your job or are incompetent in it "I disagree" would indicate fewer assumptions about roles than the other responses. Roles need to be seen positively, if our assumptions are not to cause difficulty.

12. "I somewhat agree" indicates fewer assumptions; it depends upon the woman.

13. "I somewhat agree" again says that you look to the person as a person, not as a "thing" to be labeled.

14. "I somewhat agree" recognizes that not all managers are the same. It indicates few assumptions.

Our assumptions about others and about ourselves can create difficulties for others and for ourselves. This section has been designed to make us think about those assumptions, about how we look at and listen to others, about how we view ourselves. No score is "good" or "bad," since we don't want to label ourselves or others.

The assumptions indicated in questions 1 to 14 were focused on our assumptions about age, color and role: how we make assumptions about "how old" I or another might be, about what "color" I or another might be, and about the role that I or another have taken on. These are the assumptions that usually prove significant in business and industry. There are other assumptions that tend to make difficult selves, in ourselves or in others. Sometimes they are assumptions made early in life and form part of our unconscious; they may influence our behavior without our awareness. The section below is designed to help us reflect on possibilities of unconscious motivation.

Section II: (respond from 1 to 3 as described in Section I)

15. I can't be myself in my present environment. _____

16. My emotions are not important. _____

17. I can make it in life. _____

18. I am an important part of the "world" in which I _____
live.

19. I am able to be close to others (with whom I want _____
to be close).

20. Thinking is important to me, so I do a lot of it. _____

21. I think what others expect me to think. _____

22. I feel what others expect me to feel. _____

23. Life isn't worth living. _____

24. I don't need compliments to be happy. _____

25. People don't expect compliments from me. _____

26. I must always abide by a decision I've made. _____

27. I cannot have everything I want. _____

28. I am destined to "almost make it." _____

29. I think that once I have "made my mark" things _____
will be better.

Analysis:

15. "I agree" *might* indicate an unhealthy assumption; where
have you been able to "be yourself"? It is possible that our
training or upbringing has been such that we assume that
"being ourselves" is not acceptable. We need to try doing
what we want to do and being what we want to be. Otherwise, difficulty for ourselves and/or for others.

16. "I don't agree" is indicative of a healthy response; emotions play a large part in our lives and relationships. As-

sumptions to the contrary can cripple our personal development and our relationships. To avoid difficulty we need to recognize, own and express appropriately our feelings. We are going to express them one way or the other, so it is best if we learn how to express them appropriately. We can sulk or effectively confront.

17. "I agree" is a healthy assumption. It says that we have that degree of self-confidence useful for success. There are people who have grown convinced that they need to fail. They offer difficulties for themselves and for all the rest of us (except, perhaps, those who like to "rescue" others).

18. "I agree" says that we have a feeling of "belonging," an important assumption for our self-esteem and for our relationships. Feeling that we "don't belong" presents difficulties for all concerned.

19. "I agree" says a good deal about our assumptions. People who find themselves or others difficult usually find "closeness" fearful. "Closeness" does not mean that we need to be intimate with everyone; it means that we can be intimate when we want. We need to know how to "play" with others as children do, when it is appropriate and when we want. We'll speak more of this in Chapter 4.

20. "I agree" indicates that our training and upbringing have not inhibited our thinking. Children who are told "You wouldn't understand" or "You're stupid" sometimes believe these messages. According to Claude Steiner, this may be the root of alcoholism: the best way not to think is to be drunk. An assumption that we are not to think causes difficulties for ourselves, and, sometimes, for others.

21. "I disagree" tends to point to an assumption of independence, which is often healthy. If we think what others expect us to think we may be crippling our personal development, perhaps behaving as expected rather than as is best or appropriate for us.

22. "I disagree" seems, again, to be a healthy response. To be aware of our own feelings is important; to accept them and to be able to express them appropriately is even more important if we are to be at peace with ourselves and to level with others. Feeling what others expect us to feel, simply because they expect it, can be self-destructive.

23. If our response was "I somewhat agree" or "I agree" we are probably in a depression. Our assumption is that "life isn't worth it." We may have taken seriously such messages as "Drop dead" or "Disappear" received as children. Our assumption can be very destructive to ourselves and to those around us.

24. "I agree" indicates that we are fooling ourselves. All of us need psychological support. As children, we needed to be touched and held; had such contact been denied us, we probably would not be alive today. As we get older, this physical need becomes translated into the psychological need for recognition. If we are not noticed positively (complimented), we seek to be noticed negatively (insulted or discounted). Everyone needs recognition in one way or the other.

25. "I agree" says something about yourself: you are not a person of great affection, and that is O.K. Many of us are not. The important thing is that we are satisfied about this assumption of others. If they and we are comfortable, it is fine. We shall speak more about this in Chapter 6.

26. "I agree" might indicate that your were brought up with the axiom: "You've made your bed. Now lie in it." "Always" and "never" are words proper to God. Certainly, we try to live up to our commitments and promises. To assume that we must do so at any cost could create difficulties for ourselves and for others. We need to consider what is best for all concerned, in spite of our "always" decisions.

27. "I agree" focuses on a assumption that we must always be wanting in some area of life: if we love a job, it will not pay

well; if the job pays well, we will not like it; we love our husband or wife but cannot "make love" to him or her; we do not love a man or woman but can "make love" to him or her. We may have listened too intently to lessons like "You can't have everything!" or "You can't have your cake and eat it too!" Lots of difficulties accompany this assumption.

28. "I disagree" says that you are or probably will be successful. There are some of us who try hard not to be successful: when we find ourselves on the brink of success, we act to prevent it. Like so many of our motivations, this not a conscious decision. It has been born of messages from others that we still carry about: "Try, that's all you can do," or "Well, you made the effort and that is what counts." We are like Sisyphus of the classic myth who always allowed the boulder to slip back on him as he was about to push it over the top of the cliff.

29. "I agree" is a sign of an assumption: either "I can't be happy until I do this or that" or "After I do this or that I can be happy." We assume that we must experience "something" before we can be what we want to be or do what we want to do. Frequently, we never find a way to do what has to be done "first."

These assumptions considered in Section II are at a deeper level than those reviewed in Section I. It is easier to answer for ourselves than for others. Again, the basis for many of them is the findings of Transactional Analysis (cf. E. Berne, *Beyond Times & Scripts*, Grove Press, N.Y. pp. 223–228).

Most, if not all, of us are raised with certain convictions. We have saddled ourselves with these convictions; we have accepted them on the word of others without considering their value for ourselves. These are the convictions we tried to reflect upon in this section: "Don't be yourself," "Don't be," "Try, but don't make it," "I'm stupid," "I've got to please others," "I can't be close to anyone," "I don't need others," "Others don't need me," "I am not to ask for help," and "I am not

to offer help." And there are even deeper assumptions, consid-
ered above, such as: "Once I've made a decision, that's it,"
"Something is always going to be missing in my life," and
"Things will improve if only . . ."

In our final section, let's reflect on perceptions that are
even more deeply buried, those illustrated above on pages
51–55.

Section III: As in Sections I and II respond according to your
reactions:
    1 = I disagree   2 = I somewhat agree   3 = I agree

30. Perfection is required of me.   _____

31. No one is perfect.   _____

32. I shall succeed in what I undertake.   _____

33. I'll give my best to what I undertake.   _____

34. People need time to respond.   _____

35. To move fast is to be a success.   _____

36. Emotions are unimportant in most situations.   _____

37. It is important to express our feelings appropriate-   _____
ly.

38. I need to please everyone I meet.   _____

39. I try to please my clients (students, boss, peers,   _____
etc.) all the time.

40. I know myself (my motivations, fears, goals) well.   _____

Analysis:

30. "I agree" indicates you have some similarity with George,
described above on pages 51 and 58. Somewhere along the
line we developed the conviction that we had to be perfect; as a result, we produce little, because it is not "perfect." Perhaps we need to reexamine our conviction. We

need to be content with the "best *we* can do in the *present situation!*" The alternative might be to wait for the undertaker to declare us "the best" corpse he has handled!

31. This is a cliché, so "I agree" doesn't mean much. If you said "I somewhat agree," reserving perfection to yourself, the analysis of question 30 might be appropriate.

32. "I agree" points to a good deal of confidence. You might not be successful, but that will not be because of your faulty assumptions. You might simply need additional skills, simple acquisitions in the light of your whole person.

33. "I agree" places you very close to Bertha, described on pages 52 and 59. The "I'll try" syndrome is often doomed to failure. Our assumption needs to be that we shall *do* it. Other assumptions are self-defeating.

34. "I agree" says that you have a healthy assumption: people resent being pushed. "I somewhat agree" might mean that you know some fast decision-makers who are very competent. Chances are that there are few people who do not appreciate having time to reflect. "I disagree" says that you assume speed is always important, and you may be like Bill and Charlie, described on pages 53 and 59.

35. "I agree" places you with Bill and Charlie (pages 53 and 59). Look at your behavior: do you talk fast, move fast, drum fingers, etc.? If so, you may be carrying around a faulty assumption that "hurrying is always important." It isn't.

36. "I agree" places you with Jonathan, described on pages 53 and 59. You assume that you need deal with only an intellect; but a person is more than a brain. The person involves emotions, which are important to him or her. "I somewhat agree" indicates the same kind of assumption that, on occasion, we need not pay attention to emotions. Emotions are not conclusive, nor are they to be the basis of decisions, but they always need to be considered if we are to avoid difficulty.

37. "I agree" indicates an intellectual conviction. We need to consider whether we do express our emotions appropriately. We will express them one way or the other: appropriately or inappropriately. So, why not learn to express them appropriately? Inappropriate expression of feelings is the cause of many difficulties, with ourselves as well as with others.

38. "I agree" identifies us, possibly, with Ivan, described above on pages 54 and 59. This is an assumption inculcated early in life, that "things went well" when we pleased our mother, father, teacher, etc. The problem with the assumption is that we may not do what is best for others or for ourselves, and that may reap difficulty.

39. "I agree" says what we have described in the analysis of question 38. "I somewhat agree" may be a warning signal in the light of this analysis. "I disagree" indicates that you have little problem with this assumption, and that can be healthy. Caution: there can be a healthy need to please others in our service or job.

40. "I agree" can be accurate. Only you truly know that. For most of us there are significant areas of cloudiness and uncertainty that show up when we find ourselves asking the question: "Why did I do that?" That's when we find difficulty, in ourselves or with others.

If you are like me you will move on quite quickly. But that may not be the best thing to do. One morning, after some months of being confronted with questions like these, I found an open door to myself. I dropped all appointments and retired to my room. My reflections on "perfection," "trying," "hurrying," "non-feeling," and "pleasing" brought a wealth of information, concluding in a motivation exposure of myself. I concluded my reflection at midnight that day. In a sense, I never concluded it; the findings are still with me, lighting my way to clear decisions and behaviors. Go over the forty questions and the analysis again. This may be the most valuable part of this book for you.

SURVIVAL STRATEGIES

1. Don't judge the motivation of self or of others *too hastily*. We are too complex, Don't assume or presume. Neither is usually necessary and both often trap us into phony pictures of a relationship and lead to difficult misunderstandings.
2. Work on knowing our own motivations, but don't psychoanalyze others.
3. Be aware of impressions coming at us from others. Examine those impressions before accepting them as true.
4. Have some patience with perfectionists, people in a hurry, pleasers, etc. They are often being driven. They are not often in the driver's seat. It is not patronizing to be patient. All of us need patience from others occasionally. Patience recognizes the reality of the human condition.
5. Assume the best about others, that they are honest with you, that they want to be cooperative and that they want you to succeed. Look with suspicion on negative assumptions about self or others.
6. Be ready for disappointment when we ourselves or others prove difficult. None of us can fully escape all of our hidden, destructive assumptions. Learn and get on with it in a positive manner.
7. Be sensitive to our own dangerous adjustments to difficulty: compensation, displacement, fantasy, fixation, etc. Make the choice to stop doing these things. Choose to handle the difficulty with adult thinking and with the appropriate emotional response.
8. Recognize that there may be people "out to get us," people who want to cause us problems and to create difficulties for us. But recognize also that they are few.
9. Be convinced that no one can *make* us feel good, bad, sad, glad or scared. We choose what we feel.

Summary

This may have been a hard chapter for you, whether you reflected on yourself or on another. It is not easy to see difficulties and differences as enrichments. Usually, we perceive them as problems. It is not easy to admit our presumptions about ourselves or about others. Usually they are buried. It is not easy to recognize our strategies of behavior and it is usually very difficult to reflect on the messages accepted from parents, teachers, aunts, uncles, etc., that are creating difficulties for us. It can seem a betrayal. Of course, if we thought of others, it is easier to settle on conclusions. But who can know another this well? Our conclusions for others can only be tentative.

Research has indicated that there is a whole world of unconscious drives and motivations in most of us; if we do not become aware of this world, we are at its mercy. If we can surface this world, for ourselves at least, we have a chance of controlling it, of choosing whether to be influenced by it or not in this particular situation. If we can get a glimpse of it in others, we have a better chance of understanding, tolerating and appreciating others. We do not need to become amateur psychologists; we do not want to label others or psychoanalyze others. We only want to understand so that fewer difficulties arise in our lives. That seems a reasonable expectation in the light of all the information available to us. Kindness, tolerance and appreciation can come from information about ourselves and about others.

You are probably making applications of what you have learned in many areas. I have concentrated on work life; you, if you are like many of my clients and students, are thinking about home life. Let's look at home life in the light of what we have said.

4

Difficult Relatives

Why are in-laws notorious for their notoriously disruptive influence on marriages—though not always? What makes the difference between supportive and troublesome in-laws? Why are there so many divorces? Why do other marriages thrive? Why are some children very difficult? Why are some children a joy to care for? The simple answer to all of these questions is that some relatives are difficult, while others are not. In this chapter we shall explore the differences between relatives who are difficult and relatives to whom it is a pleasure to be related.

When I was a teenager I used to hear gray-haired teachers and elders solemnly proclaim: "You can pick your friends, but you can't pick your relatives." I was intrigued, but not fully comprehending. I understood, but did not appreciate the wisdom. Now I think I do. Friends can cause heartache and anxiety; relatives can cause devastation. Relatives are deeper, more penetrating and more demanding. We may not have seen them for years, but cousins, aunts, uncles and in-laws can make demands few friends would dream of making. We can say "goodbye" to friends much easier than we can dissolve a blood relationship.

We may not think of in-laws as "blood relations," but are they not? We live with their "blood" more closely than we live with our own: we are influenced by their problems, miss dinners because of their demand on our spouse and are regularly invaded by their children only a little less than we are deprived of privacy by our "blood relatives." Unless we have "cut off" the in-laws, there is little difference between our "blood" and our "in-law." The nuclear family may not have this experience, especially if they move far from home; most of us do. Most of us find difficulty with relatives, whether they be spouse or distant cousin.

Marriage Difficulties

The first "in-law" we have to deal with (love and live with) is our own wife or husband: the spouse. According to Maude Adams (NBC "Hour Magazine" 3/30/82), the answer is to live with those we don't love and make love with those we don't live with. Her philosophy appeals to me, but I don't find it practical. Most of us live with those we love, or have committed ourselves to love for a long time, even a lifetime. The stranger in our house is our loved one; too often the problem in our life is this stranger. The question is: How do we make this stranger a friend? Or how does this friend become a lasting loved one?

The first step is the easiest, for some. *We learn to play with each other.* Teasing is often the first step to the first step. We kid, make fun of and joke with. After being in bed, unfortunately, the teasing stops. Play is forgotten. The goal has been achieved. I say "unfortunately" because if marriage is to endure, if it is to "leap tall buildings of difficulties," play is central. There can be no difficulty immune to play, no marriage survival without play. We need to play with each other.

Bills, work pressures, daily schedules, in-law pressures and inner needs can make play difficult or impossible. "Other things are more important." Time and energy are used elsewhere, because that is where "survival" is; money can be a source of anxiety and conflict: we don't have enough or we find it demanding more time than we can give to each other. We spend more time in personal relationships on the job than we do at home, and find it more *fun.* The important word is "fun." We need to play at home.

Pat and Dana, close friends of mine, were very successful in their careers. Pat is a medical technologist. Dana is into marketing. They married each other soon after college, just as their careers were beginning. They decided not to have children until careers were solidified. Because both spent most of their day on the job, arriving home in early evening, frozen dinners were agreed upon. After dinner they were too tired to spend time with each other; both had to be "up early" tomorrow.

Before their marriage Pat and Dana found time to be together; marriage, they thought, would increase that time: time for love, for play, for being with the one person they wanted to be with. Before marriage, they laughed, went to "crazy" movies, tried "little restaurants" and talked a lot. They played a lot, sometimes in bed but more often all the time. Now they work. And difficulties are surfacing more and more: more frequent arguments, more severe disagreements and less and less communication. Both feel they live with a stranger.

Do Pat and Dana want to make their marriage work? That is the first question. If they do, certain changes need to be made. In spite of bills, work schedules and careers, some reversion to pre-marriage behaviors needs to be made: time for play. Play happens between children; Pat and Dana need to be able to let go their grown-up behaviors and become children with each other. Difficulties with children are superficial and short-lived. Pat and Dana need some of that.

Where difficulties in marriage surface, play is usually absent. The partners have reverted to or discovered new diversions that do not include each other. Home is not a place to have fun; it is a place of obligations. In time, this can lead to problems: depression, alienation, separation, divorce. Unless couples play together they can't live together. The marriage certificate makes no difference.

Play is vulnerable. We need to trust. We need to open ourselves to hurt: words said, actions performed, messages clarified. All of these can hurt. To play means to trust another not to hurt us. If we can't do that, we can't play. We become distant, superficial and hostile. Play is the farthest thing from our mind and heart. We endure and tolerate, hoping things will get better.

The first step to play is communication. Couples need to

be level and straight, responsibly honest with each other. If one pontificates, that is not enough; if one listens, that is not enough. BOTH need to speak, to listen, and to know that they are heard. Feelings, as we shall explore in Chapter 6, are an important dimension of this kind of communication.

Knowing our own needs is another important dimension. We need to identify our needs, independently from the needs of the other. We need to acknowledge our needs, to own them and to be willing to accept the consequences of fulfilling them. We are not being selfish, since our honest needs are intimately involved with the partner with whom we live, play and make love. It is unfair to them if we are not able to recognize and describe the needs we expect them to fulfill. It is destructive to us not to be able to identify those needs. Play requires an acknowledgement of our own needs and an appreciation of the needs of others. Fun happens when we are able to "let go" because we trust. We cannot fulfill all the needs of another, but intimacy can fill a significant number of them, if it is honest, responsible and playful.

The second step to handling the difficult self found in marriage is *to care for each other.* "We" needs to replace "I" and "us" has to replace "me." Caring is being concerned, being interested and being somewhat selfless. Caring is what most of us experienced with our mothers and fathers: the feeling that we came first, that someone was deeply interested, that we could count on being loved. The model of caring is, in fact, very close to the parent-child relationship.

Lou, a client of mine, cared very much for Ivy. After their marriage he remembered little things: Ivy's love for flowers, her dislike of cooking every day and her deep attachment to her father. Lou gave Ivy flowers on special occasions and on no occasions. He tried to arrange for dinner "out" regularly and encouraged her to spend time with her father when possible. He remembered anniversaries, birthdays and special events Ivy planned and enjoyed. In a sense, Lou was "parenty."

Ivy loved Lou for his attentiveness, but she paid little attention to his interests: she forgot important appointments Lou had told her about, or she confused them with other appointments; she quickly forgot Lou's complaints about back pains or toothaches and was surprised when he had to seek medical attention. She asked about his day regularly, but rarely celebrated his little business successes. Ivy loved Lou, but didn't take very good care of him. In time, difficulties arose. Lou began to feel taken and was tempted to retaliate by "forgetting" occasions special to Ivy, and flowers came less frequently. Love-making lessened. Lou began to feel lonely.

The situation might have been reversed: Ivy might have been caring and Lou too busy to care. Caring is a two-way street. Most of us find it difficult to give all the time; we like to receive. Few of us are saints.

Caring can take many forms, but perhaps it is most successful when it is not needed, such as when one partner does a job that the other is usually expected to do and is perfectly capable of doing: putting out the trash, making dinner or cleaning the kitchen. The unrequested back massage, the foot rub and silent companionship can all be caring behaviors. Such caring can pave the way to play. Caring calls for effort and sensitivity: "What is needed now?" "Can I fill the need?" Difficult selves in ourselves or in others sometimes resent the effort and trample underfoot the sensitivity; then the difficult self makes its appearance.

The third step in handling the difficult self in marriage is *agreement, being compatible in value areas.* We can "play" on a one night stand, or we can play with a "mistress," whether male or female. We can even "care" in an affair, if it lasts long enough. But, if the relationship is short enough, we don't have to be compatible. Compatibility deals with basic values: fidelity, consideration, mutual support, morality, trust, responsibility and cooperation. In the long term, play and caring are important; compatibility is crucial.

Compatibility reflects the values we live by, the important issues in our lives. They have been inculcated in our conscious or unconscious by our upbringing and training, our parents, parent figures and/or our education. They are values that form the compass of our lives. Compatibility has little to do with the reasons that some give for divorce. It is deeper.

Values, of course, can change. One partner takes a training program or course and changes values that leave the other behind. This happens, on occasion, in real life. Or one partner grows to the extent that the other is left behind; this was common in the 1960's when personal growth seminars were popular. Or one partner simply by experience realizes that he or she did not marry the person he or she thought he or she married. Values were not clarified nor discussed early enough in the relationship. Discovery: incompatibility!

Jeremy was twenty-three and Zola was twenty-two when they married. Jeremy was a promising program analyst and Zola a promising interior designer. They saw their marriage as a coalition of the best and the brightest. Rose gardens were in the future. Both agreed to delay children. Both understood that frequent separations were to be expected, for business reasons. They saw reunions as all that more important. The future was exciting. It would be fun.

Jeremy received promotion after promotion; Zola did well in her profession and, after discussion with Jeremy, decided to establish her own company. She worked eighteen hours a day toward establishment, while Jeremy spent eighteen hours a day in his added responsibilities. Both rejoiced; it was what they wanted and had dreamed of. Success and the world they wanted were around the corner.

But time was marching on, and Jeremy wanted a child. Zola did not, at least, not now; too much had to be done. Jeremy felt the need for stability, a place to "come home to," "someone waiting," and a "dinner ready." Jeremy wanted a refuge from the business race. Zola felt no such needs. She was exultant over her success, feeling all of her needs fulfilled. She liked being married, especially to Jeremy, a success in himself.

A conflict of values was brewing; compatibility was at stake. Jeremy had been brought up to believe that the man was the head of the household, that the woman was to provide the home. He was doing well; what was going wrong? He didn't expect this. Zola was brought up to believe that success was important, that money made a significant difference in life. Her mother had made a home for her father, but things were different today. Couples had to pull together if success was to be assured. She couldn't understand Jeremy's flights of temper; they wouldn't talk about their concerns. They were too busy, too irritated or too tired.

The conflicts took various forms. He would proclaim that he was not interested in her work. She would retreat. He would speak of the life he expected, prologued by a description of the life his mother and father led. She would be silent. She arrived home late, more reticent and more anxious to return to work. Zola would feel guilty, inadequate to fill the needs of her marriage. She saved money, provided for the future, worked more than enough, but none of that was enough. Somewhere, she was failing.

Zola and Jeremy did not have compatible values. They brought conflict to their marriage and relationship. They cared for each other; they even played, when time allowed. They truly loved each other. Their values were different.

Play and caring are more in our control than compatibility of values. Values are deeply rooted, established about the ages of six to sixteen. Often, they are not conscious: we live by them, write by them and think by them. We rarely examine them. The success of "Values Clarification" supports our lack of reflection: we need someone to help us to surface our values.

Jeremy lost his job; he reverted to his original value system; he became depressed. Cooking, cleaning and laundry became his lot. Eventually, Jeremy questioned his assumptions. He began to appreciate Zola. His values changed. He and Zola communicated.

The process described above took much more time than is indicated; it occupied five years. The issue is that *play, caring* and *shared values* are crucial to an intimate relationship. No one of the three is indispensable. We need to play with, to care about and to share with another. Difficulty, either in another or in ourself, is the result of neglecting one or more of the three indispensables.

SURVIVAL STRATEGIES

1. *Play* with your spouse. Trust enough to be vulnerable. Make time for fun, playing Scrabble, cards, tennis , etc. Take mini-vacations together. Waste time together. Try making love in different, playful ways.
2. *Care* for your spouse without feeling "put upon." Do a job around the house that your spouse usually does, just to surprise him or her.
3. Be satisfied if you can *agree in major values*. Tolerate differences in less important areas while working toward appreciating those differences. Tolerate, for instance, a messy kitchen or workshop while trying to appreciate the work habits of your spouse. After all, things do get done eventually. Relax.
4. Allow time for growth in compatibility; a year or two is generally not enough. Hold on to your marriage like a good stock. Time, life changes, work changes can make hidden love obvious love. Remember: all of us marry strangers.

Family Difficulties

Unless we have moved far from "families," or have severed contact for some reason, in-laws impact upon marriage. I want to focus on in-laws in this section on "family difficulties."

The impact that in-laws and friends have upon marriage was first impressed upon me at a marriage performed by a politician in our nation's capital. The "minister" composed the ceremony himself, or so it seemed to me. Much of the ceremony was traditional, but at one point he asked the family members of the bride and groom to identify themselves; he then asked this group whether they supported this marriage and would do all they could to maintain it. Having received the families' commitment, he asked the same of the friends of the bride and groom.

Until that experience, it had never struck me how important relatives and friends were if husband and wife were to avoid difficulties. I have been watching for family and friend influences ever since. Perhaps I am too close to tell, but I think my own marriage has sidestepped some problems through the wisdom of our minister-politician.

There are good reasons why in-laws create difficulties, even without intending to do so: (1) there are different perceptions of the couple and of each one of the couple; (2) family "ties" are significant; (3) pride in a member of the family and expectations of the marriage union are present; (4) position in the family can be important; (5) past and present behavior can elicit in-law reaction; (6) personal success of in-laws or couple can create dynamics for difficulty; (7) significant events and how they are handled can surface problems. These are *good* reasons, since we are not brains on stilts. We have feelings, attachments and legitimate relationships—good reasons that create bad and unreal problems. On occasion, such good reasons may create real problems.

There may be unreal, phony or even corrupt reasons for undermining a marriage. Greed, incest, fraud and lust are a few. But leaving aside the seven deadly sins, let's examine some of the inner dynamics that make a marriage difficult. It seems to me that we have had enough of the obvious reasons for marriage problems created by in-laws. My intent is to look at some of the more subtle influences that are rarely identified. This is not to say that the obvious forces should be ignored, but only that they are so obvious you do not need to read a book or a chapter about them.

In-laws may have different perceptions of the couple, of each family, and of each member of the marriage. An example. Eileen came from a strong Roman Catholic family. Irving was of Jewish descent, but his family was not religious. Each family saw the other as a threat. Eileen was not the girl for Irving, in the view of Irving's family: she was alien, unacquainted with tradition, weak and indifferent to genuine culture. Eileen's family perceived Irving as irreligious, earthy and gross, alien and foreign. In the perception of the in-laws, each had little in common with the other.

Phone calls or meetings between the families were rare: a baptism, a birthday or an anniversary. But phone calls to the family were significant: when Eileen called, or Eileen's family called her, Irving was generally ignored or given token recognition. If there was a problem, Irving was always wrong. The same was true in contact betwen Irving and his family: Eileen was ignored or wrong. In-laws did little or nothing to support the marriage, because of their different perceptions of the couple. Their perceptions were too narrow to be called prejudice, but perhaps it was selective prejudice. Those who might have been a strengthening force in the marriage became a weakening force.

Prejudice was not the issue. Each family did not take the time to know and to perceive in the in-law all that the marriage partner first knew and saw. Each was dealing with a stranger.

That different perceptions are not the same as prejudice can be seen in the relationships of Patrick and Joanne. Both are Christians; both are from families of Episcopalians. Both practice their faith, on occasion. Joanne's family perceives Patrick (and his family) as lower class; Patrick's father has been a construction foreman all his life; his mother has functioned as a salesclerk or waitress when work was slow in the construction industry. Joanne's father is an investment analyst; her mother never had to work.

Joanne's family felt initially that she was marrying "below her level." They did become reconciled to the union once they became convinced of Joanne's love for Patrick and Patrick's love for Joanne. The marriage celebration went well.

In time, however, small problems started to escalate when Joanne shared them with her family: money for entertainment and vacations was meager, future planning for the baby became reason for arguments, and financing for housing caused regular conflict. Joanne's family sided with her, supporting her position and belittling Patrick: he was "incompetent," "without a career," and "demanding."

Patrick's family was less critical, but they were sympathetic to his side of the story.

Rather than the families' support, both Joanne and Patrick experienced the destructive influence of the families. Their marriage felt the impact of forces it should not have had to deal with: the forces of in-laws that created difficulty when they might have occasioned peace and tranquillity. At the root of the relationship was the perception each family had of the couple, as well as the perception each family had of the individual partner. In addition, each partner perceived each family differently: Joanne liked Patrick's family, but perceived it as insignificant; Patrick perceived Joanne's family as disapproving, haughty and snobbish. Different perceptions created difficulties that were not necessary.

Family "ties" are significant. Families can be closely knit and in-laws can expect relationships that are not practical when a member of the family is married: immediate presence in time of family need or crisis, financial sharing or time sharing. When these expectations are not met, in-laws can bring pressures on a marriage and create problems.

Pride in a member of the family and expectations of the marriage union are present. These can be realistic, healthy and life-giving. They can also cause difficulty.

An example: Salvador had studied piano since the age of seven. He had given a few limited "concerts" and was successful in the night club circuit. Peggy met him through his family; they felt she would support his career, and encouraged their relationship. After their marriage, Salvador found himself "stuck" in the night club circuit; after a child there was little time for him to further his career. His family became resentful, blaming Peggy for insufficient support and encouragement. Peggy's family could not understand the resentment, and supported her in the "battle."

The families became part of the problem, since neither supported the marriage; each supported its individual member.

Position in the family can also contribute to difficulties. In-laws may expect the youngest in the family to continue to act as a child, or the elder of the family to act as a protector. In either event, the marriage suffers, since the marriage partner does not view the spouse as "child" or "protector" of "family." The marriage partner labeled "child" or "protector" feels

called to exercise his or her expected role; the other partner
may resent such a division of "loyalties." Examples of this kind
of conflict are myriad. If this "shoe fits," each of us can paint
our own path of thickets.

Past or present behavior can elicit in-law reaction that creates marriage difficulties. Tom was a serious gambler before
marrying Marie. With the help of "Gamblers' Anonymous,"
Tom stopped his habit shortly before the marriage. Marie believes the cure was permanent, but her family's first reaction
to any sharing of marriage problems is: "Has he gone back to
gambling?" In time, Marie has to wonder herself: Has he? In-
laws have helped to erode the trust that is so essential to successful marriage. In-laws could have been supportive—"Well,
he beat one problem, so we know you can make it"—but they
were not.

To complicate the situation, Marie's job required her to
travel a great deal. Tom's family wondered "out loud" if that
was good for the marriage: "Why does she have to be away
overnight so often?" Questions were planted in Tom's mind.
In-laws could have pointed out the value of having so successful a wife, how lucky he was, how much they must appreciate
their time together. They did not. They created difficulties.

Personal success or failure can also surface difficult reactions from in-laws. Success can encourage parasites: in-laws
who expect favors, visit indefinitely or create problems out of
envy. Failure may create distances, occasion criticism or
"prove" previous expectations of the son-in-law or daughter-
in-law.

Harry was a promising data programmer with a background in accounting. Helen's family felt she had "made a
catch." As it turned out, Harry grew less and less interested in
computers and data processing; he did poorly in his job and
was eventually severed from his position. For a while he tried
to function as a consultant, but still found himself bored. He
took over the management of a "fast food" restaurant, just to
"make ends meet." Helen felt the crunch in decreased income
and shared her stress with her family, who soon decided that
Harry was a "loser." They shared their opinion with Helen,

who brought her frustration and disillusionment to Harry by way of negative criticism, barbs and discounts.

Success is less of a strain on marriage, since couples can "laugh all the way to the bank," but in-laws can find ways to make it a difficulty. Success, they might say, has made you "big-headed" and distant—"You don't have time for us anymore" or "Doesn't he or she remember where he or she came from?" Pressures are buffered by prestige and money, but they are still felt.

Events significant to the "family" can create problems for couples. In-laws may find it hard to forgive an absence from a birthday party, a funeral or a marriage and blame such "insensitivity" on their in-law: "She would have been here if it weren't for HIM!" "Lack" of attention to a dying parent, or brother or sister, is hard for an in-law geographically near to the dying person to understand: "I'm here. Why can't he or she be here? He or she makes too many demands on him or her." It is an emotional reaction. It is understandable. But the fact is that all of us have lives to live, jobs and responsibilities to maintain. Difficulty arises when "everyone should act and react as I do." Geography, responsibility, life situation and personal evaluation of need and value all contribute to the decision of a family member. But in-laws are an easy scapegoat.

Marlyn was married two years when her father was stricken with a rampant bone cancer. She had moved to another state, was pregnant and had a home and husband to care for. When she could, about twice a month, she visited her father, only to be met by brothers and sisters with such snide remarks as "Nice of you to come" or "Hello" sheathed in ice. She persisted over a six-month period, until her father died. Then she was asked to come and be reconciled with the family—to "make peace" with her eldest sister, who felt Marlyn had been negligent. Marlyn did not live in a vacuum; she shared her frustration, hurt and confusion with her husband. He, in turn, grew increasingly concerned about her pregnancy. Difficulty from in-laws was the name of the game: vicious, unintended perhaps, but potentially dangerous.

This list is not meant to be exhaustive. Probably every family on your block could add to the list. It is illustrative of how many ways in-laws can impact for good or ill on the married couple, of how important families and friends are to successful marriage. No marriage is an island any more than any individual is; married couples are part of the family fabric, so that they feel the stitches, cuts and repairs done on the fabric. We can cut the family from the fabric, and that might be healthy, or it might be impoverishing to all.

Just as there are certain qualities or dynamics that help to forestall and handle marriage difficulties, as we discussed at the beginning of this chapter, so there are dynamics that guard against in-law difficulties. Both in-laws and couples (families) need to be aware of them. The list of examples given above illustrate these dynamics.

Perception: how the in-laws see the couple, each partner in the couple as well as the members of the couple's family. This dynamic also applies to the couple and their family: how they see the in-laws. Under this heading we might include examples 1, 3 and 5 given above: (1) different perceptions among in-laws and couple (family), (3) pride in the in-laws' blood relative and expectations of the marriage, and (5) past or present behavior of all concerned and the expectations such behavior creates. In essence, all of these arise from individual perception that often becomes a kind of wish-fulfillment—"Well, what did you expect?"—for good or for ill. If the perceptions purport good, a kind of trust is communicated; if the perceptions purport ill, a kind of suspicion and/ or hostility is communicated. Receivers often "pick up" on such perceptions and act as expected.

A recent study indicates that good relationships are more likely where perceptions of the other are favorable, even when those perceptions are inaccurate objectively. Each of us, I suppose, wants to be seen as good, responsive and cooperative even if we are not. We react better to those who see us favorably. The implication for in-laws and marriage is that there will be fewer difficulties and that those difficulties that do arise will be resolved more easily when perceptions are favorable.

We need not be blind or stupid in the face of vicious behavior; as intelligent adults we cannot, with integrity, view such behavior as good. As in-laws and family, however, we can "go an extra mile" to search out the good that can be found in most of us. We can support and appeal, leaving condemnation to others.

Closeness: feelings of intimacy that arise from deep friendships, personal commitment to another and blood relationships. When a family member marries or commits himself or herself to another, he or she enters into in-law relationships through a spouse. Each family feels a closeness to their own that they may not feel for the other member of the partnership.

Closeness is illustrated in examples 2, 4 and 7 above: (2) significant family ties, (4) position in the family and (7) events significant to the family. Closeness can be central in such situations.

Parents and in-laws may feel threatened by the "loss" of a family member they have nurtured from birth. Anxiety might be fueled by their perception of the "other" to whom they are "losing" a son or daughter. Sometimes hurt and fear surface as dislike and hostility toward the "other," who, in their view, is disrupting the household.

Closeness is an outgrowth of love, and all of us must deal with it in one form or another: the death of a friend, the departure of close neighbors to a far-away city, divorce or separation, a son or daughter getting his or her own place or marrying. Grieving for a loss is the other side of the experience of love. It can be beautiful, and it is always painful, more or less.

Just as dedication can become fanaticism or love can become obsessive, so also closeness can become possessive, wanting to own exclusively and tolerating no "other" in any kind of close relationship with the person loved. Then it becomes troublesome. We possess things, not people.

Possessive closeness plays a central role in the examples recalled above; it is the kind of closeness that shuts out others, perceives hidden motives where there are none and creates difficulties where there need be none. In-laws and families afflicted with possessive closeness will find it most difficult to accept another into their enclave, into the "family" that is seen as expandable only by blood line.

At the root of possessive closeness is the fallacy that love for one person in one kind of relationship (parent-child) is lessened by love for another in another kind of relationship (husband-wife). Seen in this light, love is infinite; it need not be taken from one in order to give it to another. It may be argued that love for one lessens when we love another in the same kind of relationship: husband-wife-mistress; wife-lover-husband; still, many parents love their children equally, even though the relationships are the same kind.

Perhaps the secret for in-laws is to avoid possessive closeness—leave room for others in the lives of their children, and leave room in themselves for those their children love. Genuine closeness finds happiness in the happiness of those loved. Possessive closeness finds reasons for problems and difficulties. This applies to brothers, sisters, cousins, husbands, wives and all who comprise the family that becomes in-laws.

Control: the need to direct, order and determine the life experience of another person. This control means what it implies; don't confuse it with the control of William Schutz explained in Chapter 1. An example of this kind of control is given in illustration 6 above: (6) personal success or failure, in which in-laws create difficulties over success or failure of a married couple. At the source of the difficulty seems to be the feelings of the in-laws that they need to control what they cannot control.

In itself control can be healthy. It is a discipline we learn so that we can find happiness and satisfaction in what we have and do. We control our smoking, drinking, sleeping, etc., so that we can enjoy life; we discipline ourselves to jog, swim, eat less, etc., so that we can enjoy health and vitality. We need to control children so that they can feel comfortable in a world where there are boundaries and limits, so that they become socialized and enjoy living in a civilized culture and so that they do not hurt themselves or others. These are healthy uses of control.

Control becomes unhealthy when it doesn't know when to "let go." We cannot always control our children, since part of maturity is being autonomous. Of course, we can try to control them throughout life, and, if we are successful, they will remain children, never reaching maturity. This kind of control is used by in-laws to create difficulty. They want to control their child's happiness, so they criticize their son's wife or their daughter's husband for failure, which is supposed to bring unhappiness; or they criticize, less directly, perhaps, success, because, in their eyes, this may be a subtle insult to themselves and to their family's success; or, they are simply jealous.

In-laws are for support, not criticism; let others criticize—they'll be more than happy to do so. Families are going through constant transitions as children grow; parents change the balance of control, encouragement and withdrawal in response to the offspring's needs. When they become in-laws a major transition is required: from control and responsibility to presence and support. Maintaining control, or trying to do so, continuing to take responsibility for son or daughter will generally lead to creating difficulties. The married couple will have enough difficulties; the presence of the in-laws, their availability, their counsel when asked, their encouragement when needed and their acceptance of the other as he or she is will do much to avoid in-law difficulties and do much to help the couple resolve and overcome the real difficulties of an autonomous life.

I hope, of course, that in-laws read this chapter (and this book), since much of this section is directed to them. Even if they do not, however, couples who are seeking answers to confusing difficulties will better understand themselves and the pressures they are experiencing. Clarifying those pressures and understanding the "why" of difficulties will help them to cope, to tolerate and perhaps to resolve vague and confusing anxieties. And, after all, they might be in-laws themselves some day.

SURVIVAL STRATEGIES

1. *Be realistic.* Chances are that you, your family and your in-laws all have different expectations of your marriage. Refuse to be influenced by the expectations of your family or of your in-laws. Live your own marriage, together with your spouse, making it what you want it to be. Don't always expect support from family or in-laws.
2. Be careful of accepting support for yourself from family members if that support is only for yourself and not for your marriage. Remember: "I" is now "We" and "Me" is now "Us."
3. Discourage family members from bringing up the past in negative ways. If they negatively refer to the past mistakes of your spouse, simply suggest: "Let the past be past. Let's forget about it. Let's talk about something else."
4. Success or failure of yourself or of your spouse is your affair, not your family's or your in-laws' affair. Ignore any intrusions they make in these areas, unless they are supportive of your marriage.
5. Recognize that possessive closeness is a distorted love. Appreciate the love while tolerating the distortion without being influenced by it. The family member may not be able to love in any other way, at least for the present.

Parent-Child Difficulties

As an unmarried counselor for twelve years, I discovered that when a child was not difficult because of some physical or psychological reason, his or her difficulty often could be related to parent problems. In other words, difficult children are frequently made so because of problems parents have. Now, as a husband and father who alone cares for his child until 5 P.M. each day, my conviction has become even firmer. Most real difficulties I have with my son I create. You may not feel the same about the difficulties you have with your child, and you might be right. But have patience with me for a brief moment; let me share my thinking with you.

I am not speaking in this section about teenagers but about children from birth until twelve or so. I have found many of the insights and techniques discussed throughout this book apply equally to relating well with teenagers. Difficulties before teenage are different.

Transactional Analysis is a popular theory for understanding human behavior; much of my thinking about raising children has been influenced by it and I would like to use it as a framework here. Within each of us there are generally three ego states or bases of operation; one or the other is behind every piece of our behavior. The *Parent* in us consists of all that we learned or inferred from our elders as we grew up: how to be caring, what to care for, what to criticize, what to accept and what not to accept. Part of gaining autonomy and becoming mature is our evaluating of our *Parent* messages so as to accept them as our own or to reject them as unacceptable. We accept our *Parent* message to feed, clothe and care for our infant but reject a *Parent* message that says white Anglo-Saxons are a superior race, just as an example.

The *Adult* ego state is reason and logic, is concerned about facts, tests reality, computes probability dispassionately and digests objective information without emotion. The *Adult* begins to develop in early childhood, so it has no reference to chronological age. The mature individual uses the *Adult* as the executor of his or her personality, depending on it to properly use the other ego states. This idea is central to my thinking about Parent-Child problems. I shall refer back to it later.

The *Child* ego state is joy, wonder, self-centeredness, stubbornness, love, trust, fear, anger and manipulation: all that we see happen in a child up until the ages of five or seven. It includes our childhood behavior and patterns of response to others. Like the Parent, it is not fully conscious, and maturity calls us to examine it just as we examine our Parent. This is the barest of outlines of ego states, but adequate, I think, for our present needs. (For more, refer to M. James and D. Jongeward, *Born To Win*, Addison-Wesley, 1973, especially Chapter 2.)

Before our children enter the teenage phase the weight of our relationships rests with us. We are the adults, the mature people who have been entrusted with the child. When our children become fifteen and sixteen, some of that weight is transferred, at least in the sense that we do not usually have the control or influence that is appropriate with younger children. Before the teenage phase we need to think and judge for ourselves as well as for our children.

Parents need to take their own needs seriously. Being parents does not exempt us from being human. We need to pursue our interests, to relax, to have time alone and to enjoy life in our unique way. With a child to care for, it is dangerous to deny personal needs; in the long run, we may resent the child for depriving us, for imprisoning us, for frustrating us. Difficulty arises when we take such feelings out on the child, directly or indirectly: we become angry when we should be patient, we ignore when we should be attentive, we discipline when we should teach. We take our resentment out on our son or daughter just as we would take out our resentment on anyone who would constantly frustrate us.

In our quieter moments, perhaps after the child has gone to bed, we ask: "Why do we do that? Why did I behave that way?" The answer is usually complex. Our *Parent* ego state wants to nurture and protect our child; it is constantly telling us how things should be done, what we are expected to do; it is also constantly berating us if we do not live up to its expectations. If it is a healthy Parent, it is also nurturing us for what we do, and that helps to avoid difficulties; if it is unhealthy, it is regularly making us feel inadequate. If it is healthy, it encourages us to take care of ourselves; if it is unhealthy, it scolds us for our self-concern. An unhealthy *Parent* creates difficulties because it will not allow us to fill our own needs, and, since we are human, this leads to frustration which we may vent on the child. He or she becomes upset, our frustration is escalated and uproar ensues.

We need to recognize that we are parents, the grown-ups and adults of the relationship, and behave accordingly. Sometimes our *Child* ego state tends to dominate our child rearing; studies have indicated that this is often the reason for child abuse. We act vengefully: the child hits, we hit back; the child hits harder, we hit harder; the child screams, we scream louder, etc. Because we are stronger the child loses, sometimes fatally. Our *Child* has beaten our child because there was no *Adult* present. This is part of the complex answer promised above: when we become frustrated enough because of our own *Parent* "beating" on us, our own *Child* rebels at not having its needs satisfied and we take it out on the child. Result: difficulty. We have become a *Child* raising a child; what can we expect but difficulty? In our quieter moments, all of us acknowledge this, especially when we are not dealing with our own children.

We need to accept our own competence to deal with our child. We need to believe that we know what we are doing, that we are able to do what needs to be done, and we should not be repentant about doing our best. Mostly, this means that we have a good self-esteem. When the *Parent* within us criticizes, when it cynically points out what we "should have done," when we find ourselves disliking ourselves, we become dangerous to our child. We are angry, disappointed in ourselves and anxious about our ability to act properly in the future. Then we are at the mercy of an unhealthy *Parent*. If we reflect back on our own childhood we shall probably find that our parents, teachers, older brothers or sisters, grandparents, etc., showed little respect for our feelings, thoughts or needs. We may have even been belittled. We need to resist the temptation to "continue the tradition" with our own child. We need to examine the validity of those unhealthy messages communicated, often unintentionally, by our *Parent* figures.

Our reluctance to make such a serious examination of our "head" is often due to our fear of finding that those whom we love so much hurt us, that they restricted our awareness, our spontaneity and our autonomy. And we don't want to lose our idols, and legitimately so. We need not be reluctant. The fact is that if we are restricted, if we feel incompetent, if our *Parent*

or *Child* is unhealthy, ninety percent of the time WE are responsible. Each child interprets the messages he or she receives from elders as he or she chooses. Parents can say the
same thing to two of their children and one child will interpret
it one way, the other will interpret it another way. "You'll poi-
son yourself one day" may be interpreted by one child to mean
that he or she will commit suicide, while to another child it will
mean that "Mommy loves me and doesn't want me to hurt myself." In other words, we parents need not be paranoid about
every word that comes from our mouth: children interpret in
their own way, very, very individually. In examining our own
Parent, therefore, we are examining our own interpretations,
not sitting in judgment of our parent figures.

The *Child* in us can also contribute to our feelings of incompetence. Remember, it is self-centered and stubborn, as
well as joyous and filled with wonder. It can be vindictive as
well as loving. Our child can "hook" our *Child*, so that we feel
incapable of coping. "Do that again and I'll smack you!" in a
high-pitched voice can be our *Child* responding to our child;
"Shut up!" in resounding decibels is the *Child* in the parent responding to the child. In time, we parents begin to think that
we can control our child only with shouts and threats. Then
our *Child* has won; we have a *Child* raising a child. A sure indi-
cation is the parents' lament: "He or she doesn't understand
anything else." In other words, we don't know what else to do;
we feel incompetent.

But what is there to do? We need to consciously and carefully sift through our own *Parent* and *Child* convictions, assumptions that we usually act on without thinking. We need to
make our *Parent* and *Child* serve our *Adult*, if we are to avoid
or handle difficulties with children. The *Adult* in each of us
needs to become the choice-maker: it needs to have sufficient
control to determine when the *Parent* may act appropriately
and when the *Child* may act appropriately. The *Adult* does
not have feelings, so the *Parent* needs to care for, show love
and protect, and the *Child* needs to play, enjoy and relate at a
child's level. There are times when parents need to react in

these ways, but it is important that they do it consciously through their own *Adult*; parents need an awareness of what they are doing with their children and why they are doing it. At first this takes effort; in time it becomes second nature. At all times, however, in my experience, we need occasionally to reflect on where we are, what ego state is in command, so that we can evaluate our response. This may sound troublesome and clinical, but the alternative is even more troublesome and can be more clinical; difficulty with our children grows with them: little difficulties become big difficulties; small difficulties can grow bigger than both of us.

A parent's control of their own *Parent, Adult* and *Child* is central to avoiding difficulties with children and to handling them when they arise. There are other factors, such as fatigue, sickness, impatience, etc., but all, it seems to me, are secondary to our parents' need to know and to discipline ourselves.

Children work at growing both physically and psychologically. No matter how knowledgeable and disciplined parents are, growth always has its own problems. The solution to many such normal problems is the child's own self-esteem, and parents can help children to develop healthy self-esteem, good self-images. We need to be supportive, define limitations and listen attentively to children's needs for attention and encouragement. Without unduly ignoring our own needs, we need to be in our *Adult* when children are children.

This is particularly true when the child is between the ages of five and seven because at this age the child's problem of self-identification is most intense; he or she is busy answering the question "Who am I?" Problems and difficulties at this age are often growth-created, not parent-created. They are very real for the child. He or she is surrounded by a myriad of models: elders, grandparents, parents, television personalities, fictional characters and comic heroes. Which of these is he or she supposed to be like? The child needs to know. We need to listen and to be available, to communicate supportive and growth-giving messages, to *Parent* when appropriate and to *Child* when appropriate—but always to be *Adult*.

SURVIVAL STRATEGIES

1. Don't behave like a supermom or superpop. Recognize your own needs: make time to be alone, make time to be alone together with your spouse, make time to pursue a hobby or interest without the children.
2. Be satisfied with doing your best to care for your children. Don't "beat" on yourself. Be confident in your ability.
3. Know when you are using your *Parent, Adult* or *Child* ego state. Chances are that you will then be using them appropriately.

Summary

Difficult relatives come in different sizes and shapes. We have reflected on marriage difficulties, family difficulties (in-laws) and parent-child difficulties, reviewing some of the major dynamics that give rise to difficulties in these key relationships and suggesting ways of handling these dynamics.

A satisfying and lasting marriage seems to call for the couple to play with each other, to care for each other and to be compatible. In the language of Transactional Analysis, they need to relate *Child* to *Child* in play, to relate *Parent* to *Child* (mutually) in taking care of each other and to relate *Parent* to *Parent* in agreeing on values and priorities that are compatible (cf. L.W. and H.S. Boyd, "A Transactional Model for Relationship Counseling," *Transactional Analysis Journal*, Vol. 11, No. 2, April 1981, pp. 142–146).

In-law difficulties often arise out of the different perceptions, the different ways of seeing of each set of in-laws. We need to create a culture in which in-laws are seen as responsible for supporting and nurturing a marriage as long as honesty and integrity allow. Perception, closeness and control seem to be the most active dynamics in in-law relationships. To avoid and to handle difficulties perception needs to be positive, closeness to be realistic and control to be caring.

Parent-child difficulties, in my counseling and personal experience, are largely parent-created. We make the mistake of ignoring our own needs as parents to the breaking point; we forget our position as grown-ups and adults as well as the wisdom that should come with those roles; we allow ourselves to feel frustrated at our perceived incompetence. In any case, we take out our frustration on the child and create difficulties. In Transactional Analysis terms, our *Adult* has insufficient control over our *Parent* and *Child*. We need to raise our child with our *Parent* as well as with our *Child*, but only under *Adult* supervision.

This is not to say that children don't have real problems and difficulties that arise from their growing up. I only suggest that we parents sometimes create a lot more problems than are necessary in the growth process.

We need now to move out of the family and home and into the workplace. Family difficulties can cost dearly, but work problems are also costly. They can, perhaps too often, create family difficulties. In the next chapter we shall reflect on difficulties that sometimes arise where we spend more than one-third of our vital, adult years.

5

Work Difficulties

When I asked Josephine what "work" meant to her she said, "Where I am most of my time. What I want to enjoy. How I make my living. What I want to do." Josephine, a secretary, obviously enjoyed her work. Her tone was positive, her answers factual and her attitude was childlike. She enjoyed her work. She was pleased that I had asked her my question.

Nadine was different. She was a bank supervisor: "I'm underpaid, undervalued and I'm tired of seeing a gun in my face. I've been through three holdups. Work to me is a drudge, a necessary evil, a punishment for being poor. I guess not every job is like this, but I wish I could find one that isn't."

Our first reaction might be to attribute the different reactions to the two very different kinds of jobs. Nadine was in a threatening position, while Josephine was not. That may well be part of the answer. Surveys and research indicate that it is only *part*. Ten years ago, when the economy was good, a study of three thousand workers in sixteen organizations indicated that forty-three percent of non-professional white collar workers and twenty-four percent of blue collar workers would choose similar work again, if they had the choice. The deduction is obvious: most of our work force is unhappy. (Study of the Roper organization, based on a survey of Detroit workers and Massachusetts educators; workshop conducted by Drake-Beam and Associates, N.Y.)

The Roper study indicated that professionals (college professors, lawyers and administrative educators) enjoyed their work; skilled workers (auto, steel, textile) did not enjoy their work. Unskilled workers dropped below the twenty-four percent contentment level noted above. A first glance seems to indicate that workers with most control over their work and its environment are most satisfied. The less control we have over the use of our time and energy, the less our satisfaction. The less we feel we are using our talents, the more automated we feel, the less our satisfaction with work.

I have used work examples in Chapters 1 and 2 to illustrate points about common difficulties that we experience. Many of our difficulties arise from work relationships; many also arise from family relationships, as indicated in Chapter 4. We do, however, spend the bulk of our time in a work situation, so I feel it is now time to look directly at *work*. In this chapter I want to focus on those elements in the work situation that create difficulty. We shall look not at the people in the situation, which we have done so far, but at the situation itself.

The Design of a Job

A job can be designed for frustration when its place, function and contribution to the total product is fuzzy or unknown. The design engineer needs to know the end result of his labor. To avoid difficulty in the work situation, a worker needs to do a *complete piece of work in and of itself.* Pride, motivation and interest are at stake.

Secretaries and clerical workers are prime targets of frustration, in the sense of feeling unimportant. Roseann, a good (not exceptional) secretary in a small corporation, worked hard at her job. She was frequently told how valuable her services were, but never told *why.* She did not understand how her work fitted into the total product the company produced. Everything seemed to be urgent, but nothing complete. A worker needs to feel that in some way he or she has completed a good piece of work in and of itself, a piece of work that contributes to the total product of the company or organization— in itself. He or she needs to have a sense of completion. Any other kind of job is doomed to cause frustration and the eventual loss of a worker.

Difficulties such as poor workmanship, apathy and care-lessness can often be traced to a "bit" or assembly line job de-sign: each worker does a "bit," an isolated piece of the total product. He or she cannot be proud of the end product, since he or she did only a bit on the line. As a result, the individual worker does not take pride in the quality of the work pro-duced. No *one* cares, except the accounting department that looks at the cost of massive retooling.

The same kind of disinterest in quality can be found in the professions, institutions and governments that all of us deal with at one time or another. The medical student graduates without an appreciation of history, culture or the qualifications that used to make an educated man; the individual health technician functions without sincere contact with others on the hospital staff; the college professor teaches in his room as though on a prairie where only he and his current students ex-ist; the minister conducts his parish as though no other churches existed for a thousand miles. Difficulties result: the medical doctor feels empty of education and lives the narrow life of medicine; the hospital patient is given improper or indif-ferent treatment; the college graduate is graduated half-edu-cated and finds frustration in his or her limitations; the parishioner is deprived of services and experiences of other parishes. The list could go on and on, ways in which the ten-derer of service and the receiver of service suffer difficulty be-cause of the design of a job. No one feels responsible for the total task because no one's job is a complete piece of work in itself. We are allowed to do and to know only so much. Perhaps some jobs, such as healing the sick, can sometimes be too big for one person, but a sense of completeness can be shared by communication and active cooperation among all involved. We shall reflect more on this in the next section of the chapter.

A second element that helps to avoid job difficulty has to do with the amount of *control the worker has over his or her job.* The way a job is to be done, the time it involves and its relationship to other jobs and people are included in the area of control.

Perhaps a blatant example is best for our purpose of illustration. Morris is a very talented craftsman, a worker in metals and wood. His job at the factory is the fashioning of molds to precise measurements. To do his job he needs raw materials that are stored in a building across the factory yard. Morris is expected to transport his own raw material to his machine. He has asked several times that provision be made near his machine for the storage of the raw materials and has even designed a layout whereby this could be done without infringing on the space of others. Morris feels that he could then use his proper talents more effectively and produce more work. His requests have regularly been ignored. He feels little control over his job.

Generally, the more control a worker has over his job the better the job is designed and the fewer difficulties it presents. The less control built into a job design, the more difficulties are likely to arise, surfacing in worker indifference, low morale and frequent turnover. This is probably why the Roper survey indicated that professionals tend to be more satisfied with their jobs than non-professionals.

Valerie is a clerk typist at a community college, a skilled typist and skilled in the use of the word processor. She is responsible for assembling the catalogue each semester. Her supervisor insists on a typed copy of the catalogue. Valerie has repeatedly pointed out that she could do the task more quickly and more easily on the word processor, and each time the supervisor has responded that she wanted good typed copy. There is a slight quality difference between the typed copy and the word processor printer copy, but Valerie has never understood why this slight difference is important and her supervisor has never really talked to her about it. Valerie feels little control over her job. She might be wrong, but she doesn't know why. She has a difficulty.

People need to feel responsible for the outcome of their job. In general, professionals feel such responsibility; doctors, professors, and lawyers tend to be able to determine how their job will be done. While bound by professional standards, they can often control their time, work load and techniques used in the fulfillment of their tasks. Assuming that the non-professional understands his or her job and is skilled in its execution, supervisors can help to avoid difficulties by working with workers so that workers do as much as they can to control their task without losing quality or quantity desired by management.

A third key element in a good job design is feedback: the *worker, by design, receives direct information on his or her performance from those who use his or her product or services.* Every good supervisor knows that workers function better when they receive information from the supervisor about their performance; this is simply good supervision. Positive compliments, when they are sincere and honest, especially help to motivate the worker and to improve the quality of the work. Direct information from the user of the product or service goes further. It imparts to the worker feelings of pride and importance and, sometimes, the need for improvement from those who need what he or she does.

Peter is a car mechanic in a large agency. He is highly respected by his boss and many of the other mechanics for his expertise. During the last five years the agency instituted a program of evaluation for the service they give to their customers' cars. It is a written evaluation given to the customer with the bill. It asks questions such as whether the customer is satisfied with the repairs done, the service given, whether the car was ready when promised and what they would like to see improved in the service department. About twenty percent of the customers take the trouble to complete and return the evaluation, but Peter has never seen one. Evaluations are sent to the manager, not to Peter; the customer doesn't know Peter worked on his car. Even if the manager shared the evaluations with Peter and the other mechanics, it wouldn't mean much. No one mechanic could identify the feedback as pertaining to him or her. We are less concerned about a job, more vulnerable to indifference and dissatisfaction when we are lost in a crowd.

Feedback is always a little painful when it calls for possible improvement, but as part of a job design it is an effective way to correct little difficulties before they become big ones.

Where feedback is expected, in fact, it becomes less feared and painful.

People want to feel useful and appreciated by their employer as well as by those they serve. Money is important, benefits are important, but, as Herzberg's studies indicate, they soon lose their motivating force for satisfaction. We need to be able to stand behind our work. When we can do so we focus on real difficulties rather than those phony difficulties of self-doubt and apathy. We can focus on growth and improvement.

An Approach to a Solution

Productive job design suggests that a worker (1) be and feel responsible for his or her task, (2) have a significant degree of control over how the task is done, and (3) receive significant information about the value and professionalism of his or her job. Absence of any of these three elements creates potential job dissatisfaction and employee difficulty.

For the past twelve years Simon has been an employee of a firm in Japan. Ten years ago his boss and supervisors toured the United States, focusing on American productivity and the concepts of American behavioral scientists. Upon their return, Simon noticed a slight change: they seemed more concerned with Simon's view of his job, how it might be improved or changed for greater production. After a few months Simon was invited to join a group called the "Quality Circle," whose task was to utilize the information and views of employees about their day to day tasks. Simon accepted the invitation. He had been satisfied before, to some extent, but now felt privileged and honored to be called upon for suggestions. It was not without some doubt and trepidation that he accepted the invitation. "Was it sincere? Was it a trick? Was he being 'set-up'?" were questions that ran through his mind. In addition, he had not heard of such groups in American industry. "What did his supervisor have in mind?"

Today Simon knows that there were no such groups in America. His boss and supervisors had taken the behavioral science concepts they had learned in America and applied them to the real work situation. They were pioneers, establishing the first "Quality Circles" that would increase worker satisfaction and decrease work difficulties by giving total work output, work control and performance evaluation to the hands of the worker. Decisions of significance remained with Simon's superiors, but within that context he and his fellow workers could influence their daily activity.

A Quality Circle is composed of a group of employees doing similar work; they join the group, usually numbering eight to ten, voluntarily with the approval of senior management. Meeting once a week for an hour on company time, they work with their supervisor as a group leader on ways to improve the quality and quantity of their work. The supervisor and the group members both receive training in group dynamics, decision making, problem solving and effective communication until they are operating as a team, rather than as "boss" and "subordinates." Union leaders are encouraged to attend. Since the group is operating under the approval of senior management, the company's management and technical resources are at its disposal. Many such circles, including Simon's, have profited the company thousands of dollars during the first ten weeks of operation (cf. Ed Yager, "Quality Circles: A Tool for the '80's," *Training and Development Journal*, August 1980, pp. 60–62).

Quality Circles are now used in a number of American companies. They are successful because they are based upon significant findings of the behavioral sciences.

All involved in change need to be involved in its initiation. Without the understanding and approval of senior management, no change is likely to be successful, except, perhaps, revolution in which power is torn out of the hands of the powerful. An example of failure brought about by ignoring this basic principle is the Second Vatican Council of the Roman Catholic Church. After twenty years it seems clear that the senior management of the Church, the Pope and bishops, did not understand nor truly approve of the changes voted by the Council; implications were not fully appreciated nor contemplated. Only the superficial changes from Latin to vernacular, from clerical emphasis to lay emphasis, and from triumphalism to poverty were acknowledged, without a thorough understanding of the ramifications such changes would require. When such ramifications were logically demanded by Church members, they were met by indifference and rejection by senior management. Senior management was not genuinely involved in the initiation of the change suggested.

The other side of this coin is that *people should not be forced to change,* especially if the change is designed to be permanent; *they need to be involved in changes in their job and work close to them.* This means that Quality Circles need to be voluntary but inclusive, providing for those who do not want to take part in the Circle in other, honorable ways.

Leo was sixty years of age and an employee of an American industrial firm for thirty years when the concept of Quality Circles was introduced. He felt most uncomfortable with the notion, seeing no reason for it even after being exposed to an orientation session. "We're doing all right without all of this stuff, and it seems like it will be a waste of time!" was his reaction. His supervisors and the company trainers spoke with him, asking him to "at least try to be part of the Circle for a week or two." Under such duress, he did try, but found that, from his perception, it was a session for complaints. Leo was allowed to withdraw, joining a group of workers not involved in Quality Circles.

Some "Leos" might have changed after a few exposures to the Quality Circles, and they would have continued with the group. This Leo did not. The point is that just as senior management must support the effort, so must the members of the Circles be there voluntarily. Workers who do not participate are not penalized, but they need to change their position in the work force. Circles that are not voluntary become detrimental and difficult; that is quite the opposite to what is intended. In essence, we cannot and should not *force* people to change. Change is possible and stable only when undertaken voluntarily.

Work should have its own motivation and be enriching.

We have spoken about this need to some extent in the first part of this chapter: workers need to take pride in their product, have reasonable control over their task and receive significant feedback from their "customers." Quality Circles can be a vehicle for creating an environment in which the worker can experience the fulfillment of these needs.

Dan worked only for his paycheck; he had little choice, since it was the only visible sign of his efforts. He was one of several quality control supervisors in an oil refinery. Before Dan was born the criteria for oil quality were established, modified slightly by government intervention every now and then. As a chemical engineer, Dan was knowledgeable about the levels of oil quality, but he was never asked his opinion. His routine was set, allowing him little or no control over his daily operation; he was to follow the "guidelines." Except for an occasional remark from neighbors about the company he served, he received no feedback about the product for which he felt responsible.

During the first few years of his employment Dan was satisfied. He was happy to have a significant job and enjoyed the responsibility. Only after his preliminary satisfaction did he begin to think, reflecting on better ways to accomplish the task he had been hired to do, how to save time and effort and how to be more accurate in his evaluation. Since he received no feedback, except a perfunctory evaluation on an annual basis, he could not be sure that any of his ideas were sound. When he did make suggestions they were met with indifference or hostility. In time, Dan became a difficult person. He settled to work for his paycheck. Local management relaxed when Dan retired.

QUESTION: Could Quality Circles or similar approaches have better utilized Dan's talents, or was he a troublemaker?

ANSWER: How can we know if we do not modify job structures to be more human and solicitous of employees' suggestions?

Difficulties banished leave questions unanswered. Dan left his job with feelings of dissatisfaction and disappointment. He had grown little and suffered much from the imposed routine

years helped him to see that there were other ways to get things done. He and his men volunteered for a Quality Circle. In time, Chris began to hear what his men had been saying for years and "screwed up" his courage to try to be less directive. He still got the job done on schedule, but the turnover in his department dropped considerably. He found his men "less difficult," and they found some enrichment and reasons to stay in Chris' department.

SURVIVAL STRATEGIES

1. If you are "caught" in an unsatisfying job, think of ways it could be made more satisfying. Make suggestions to the appropriate people at the appropriate times. Don't "discount" by saying: "Nothing would help this lousy job."
2. If you are unsuccessful in making a job satisfying after a reasonable period of time, consider new employment. New employment might not be the answer to job satisfaction, but you have nothing to lose after doing all you could to find satisfaction in your job. Regardless of benefits or seniority, regardless of family concerns, you need to live your life. You need to find fulfillment. You will be no good to anyone if you "stay on." But remember: a change does not guarantee that things will be better or more satisfying. Have courage: it is never too late if you move cautiously and with reasonable contacts. Those who love you will support you (see Chapter 9).
3. Recognize the impact of an unsatisfying job on people with whom you work and with whom you have difficulty. It will help you to be less angry and upset with conflict. Neither you nor others are always to blame. The construct of the job may create difficult people. Change the job, one way or the other.
4. Don't support gripe sessions. Generally they only increase dissatisfaction and offer no constructive rewards.

Types of Management and Difficult People

Management can make people difficult, even when a job is in itself satisfying and fulfilling. As I indicated above, there seems to be some correlation between management style and communication style. The more directive the management style, the more communication is one-way: from "up" to "down"; the more cooperative the management style, the more communication is two-way, speaking, hearing and responding. Still, there is no communication that does not occasion a response of some kind: the sender of the message is affected by what he or she says or writes and the receiver accepts the message in his or her own way, even when no verbal or written response is expected or given. The message of the sender is stamped with his or her personality and the receiver takes in the message through the filter of his or her own personality. I suggest that it is less the management style that creates difficult people than it is the communication style that inevitably accompanies the particular management style.

Some students of management and the behavioral sciences have suggested four different patterns of management and their accompanying communication pattern: (1) a developmental pattern that habitually has concern for the company and its product as well as for the people involved in producing the product, (2) a controlling pattern that is regularly more concerned about getting the job done according to "the book" and his or her own ideas than about the doers of the job, (3) a relinquishing pattern which is more concerned about pleasing others than about doing the job well, and (4) a defensive pattern that has little concern about doing a good job or valuing employees but is focused on "fire fighting" and evading responsibility.

A *developmental manager* places high value on both the organization and the people in it. Such managers do not like to risk hurting or losing business or people. They seem to communicate by *informing* and *exploring*. They naturally surface alternative ideas and new facts that can contribute to decision making and problem solving. They mutually explore the ideas of others and identify experiences of others as well as of themselves that could have bearing on an issue. Communication is essentially two-way.

Carl, a manager in a small manufacturing firm, seems to have a developmental pattern of management and its accompanying communication style. Whenever production or marketing, for instance, meets a snag, he rarely gives an immediate solution. More often he calls in the production or marketing people and discusses the problem with them, sharing his observations but also asking for their perceptions and ways to assure that the problem won't reoccur. People like to work for Carl, rarely leaving the company except for extraordinary reasons. Carl knows there are some difficult people in the company, and he tries to help them become more content. One thing seems fairly certain: Carl's style didn't create the difficult people.

A *controlling manager* values stipulated procedures and his personal ideas. He wants things done only one way: "his" way. Controlling managers have little time for creativity or experimentation: "We've always done it this way" is carved on his office door. Creative people tend to anger or to confuse such managers. They communicate with *persuasion* and *enforcement*. Not being interested in the ideas of others or in alternative ways of doing things, their initial communication on most issues is an attempt to persuade the other to approach a task in a specified way. If they meet with resistance, controlling managers move on to enforcing their instructions by pointing out unpleasant consequences if others do not act as expected. Communication is one-way.

Alan is a businessman who has been quite successful; he owns a small chain of men's clothing stores. His message to his managers is quite clear: "Do business the way I've done business, the way you've been trained to do it in our training sessions. Sell good merchandise for a profit. Follow the 'book.'" His managers are loyal to Alan because he pays well, has a profit sharing plan for them and gives frequent bonuses. On the other hand, some of the managers find Alan difficult and occasionally take out their frustration on the sales personnel. They find sales people hard to keep. They are not interested in the ideas of the sales personnel any more than Alan is interested in their own ideas. Alan's stores have more than their share of difficult people. Employees feel stifled and, sometimes, threatened.

A *relinquishing manager* is driven to please others, even to the extent of blaming himself when things go wrong because he followed the wishes of another against his better judgment. He is willing to do more than cooperate. His communication style is first *accommodating* and then *complying*. He tries, first, to fit in the ideas and wishes of others with his own, without giving up all of his own convictions. When this is not enough, relinquishing managers submit completely to another's viewpoint while still accepting involvement and responsibility for the action or lack of action with which they disagree. Communication is one-way: from others to the relinquishing manager.

Stan was a relinquishing manager until he learned his lesson and moved to another job. He tells the story like this: "Yeah, I *was* manager of the credit department at Bunnhill's for five years. I was let go because of allowing credit to poor risks. It was during the years when business was poor all over and old Bunnhill felt I was being too selective about whom I let have credit. So, one day he called me into that big office of his and convinced me to loosen up on our guidelines. He treated me like a brother, even though I told him, at least at first, that I thought we ought to keep things tight. But, what the heck—he was the boss! It was his money. So, I gave out credit as though it was going out of style, even though I knew we were taking awful chances. Well, to make a long story short, about a year later one of the vice presidents called me to his office and told me I was through, that I hadn't handled the awarding of credit in a responsible way." Stan left a lot of difficult people at Bunnhill's: the credit department employees who felt confused about what was expected of them, an irate Mr. Bunnhill and several irritated vice presidents who "had to clean up the mess." Confusion, hostility and indifference usually surround and follow the relinquishing manager. It looks as though he or she doesn't care, so why should others?

A *defensive manager* is really not a manager in any acceptable sense of the term. He or she does not manage; such managers primarily are driven by survival, principally their own. They do not plan, organize, implement or control the four basic functions of management. They do try to keep things running smoothly by ignoring or temporarily short circuiting problems. They do not really communicate, their first reaction to a situation being to *withdraw* if possible, to escape the problem solving process and to cease to contribute or to ask for ideas from others. If they are pushed to be a part of the decision making process, they often respond with an *emotional outburst*, usually at the person pushing rather than at the situation at hand. The only communication is one-way: "Leave me alone." Each of us may feel this way at one time or another, but most of us, thankfully, do not try to manage anything with such an approach. Yet all of us know that such "managers" do exist.

Josette was one. For five years she held the post of superintendent of schools in a county school system. After only a few months on the job she felt inadequate for the task, but decided to do her best. She muddled through with little effective organization or planning; things just "rolled along" as they had always done, problems surfacing like bubbles from a sunken tanker. She spent much of her time trying to handle problems with the school board and in the individual schools until frustration mounted on all sides. She began to be "unavailable," "in a meeting," or "on the road today." When principals or supervisors did catch up with her they found her irritable and difficult; at times she was insulting, thereby helping to create more difficult people in the system. Soon no one wanted to approach her. A sigh of relief greeted her resignation.

114 *Dealing with Difficult People*

SURVIVAL STRATEGIES

If you are a manager or supervisor reflect on how responsible you are for creating difficulties for yourself. Take some risks: listen to your employees and their ideas, as stupid and as "ancient" as they may be. You may know they are infantile and ineffective. But listen. Then, make decisions *with* them. You have only a few minutes to lose now, but many hours to gain in the future. People work better *with* you than *for* you. Become a developmental manager for six months. Then do what you will. Things may get worse before they get better, but persevere. Work with your superior, so that he or she knows what is going on.

Fellow Workers and Difficulties

Difficult workers are made, not born. The job might be satisfying and interesting, challenging us just enough to be fun and attractive. Our experience of management might be good; management listens to our ideas, implements some of them, and it is helpful when we feel stymied now and again. Our organization might have Quality Circles and a significant reward system; it might be doing all it can to attract and to keep good workers and what it is doing is quite successful. But we still have to put up with difficult people.

Difficult people are made difficult by other people, if not always, at least frequently. We develop habits, ways of relating to each other, from our family and friends, and those habits are not always healthy. It seems almost endemic to Americans to "put others down." We learn to do this at home and in school as "kidding," almost as proof that we are close to another because we can "put them down" in fun and everyone understands, generally responding with a laugh or guffaw. There even seem to be some individuals who cannot relate to others except in this negative fashion: "Hi, Winnie; see you got a new dress. Did you go to the flea market over the weekend? Ha!

Ha!" or "Hello Bob. That was a great report you gave today. Who did it for you? Ha! Ha!" The unfortunate fact is that most of us are taken in by such "kidding," since it is so widespread, and we join in the laughter at ourselves or at others. Another unfortunate fact is that such "busting" is phony currency: it promises to buy closeness but never delivers. I shall call this exercise in futility "discounting," following the tradition of Transactional Analysis (cf. J.L. Schiff, *Cathexis Reader*, Harper & Row, N.Y., 1975, pp. 14–18).

When we discount another or ourselves we minimize or ignore some aspect of another, of ourselves or of a situation. For example:

Self-discount: "I couldn't learn a trade; I'm too dumb!"

Mother to child after a fall: "Get up, clumsy! When are you going to stop falling over your own feet?"

A situation: "Nothing could help this company. It's dead!"

Boss to secretary: "Miss Jones, did you type these letters with your toes again!"

Any of these statements might be true or at least be close to true. What makes them discounts is that they minimize or ignore another, oneself or a situation before looking at other factors involved and before attempting any serious problem solving. They are designed to close an issue that hasn't been opened. They are designed to evoke hopelessness. If the issue is serious, discounts can make others feel difficult or encourage others to perceive the discounter as difficult. At the very least, even when issues are not serious, they create an environment in which it is difficult to do good work. We never know when to prepare for the "zing."

While Karen was growing up she was often discounted; it was part of the family culture, one of the ways they showed how "close" they were: "You wouldn't understand. You're too little," or "Can't you ever get anything right? Let me do it," or

"She's cute, but, boy, is she stupid!" She never thought about it much, at least consciously, but as time went on she became more and more self-conscious and insecure. In spite of these feelings she became a legal assistant and secured a position with a law firm. Throughout school she had few friends and seemed to have little good to say about her classmates. They avoided her, some saying that she was difficult to get to know. She always seemed to have a wisecrack. Her co-workers in the firm did not like to work with her because she seemed so negative all the time. She was tolerated until she moved on to make work miserable for others in other places.

Karen used discounts to hide her own insecurity, not to make life difficult for herself or others. But intentions don't count when we look at behavior and its consequences. Others had made her a difficult person and she was inclined to make more difficult people, to pass on the bad experience. She didn't know how else to behave.

The tragedy is that discounts are done outside of our awareness and impede our thinking without our being conscious of it. In short, we do not know what we are doing. In this sense, they are like "games" as we discussed them in Chapter 2. We need help to discover what we are doing. Others can help, and so can books such as this.

There are *areas* in which we discount and there are *levels* at which we discount. We can discount in the areas of feelings, problems and options. We can discount on the levels of existence, significance, alternatives and personal capability. Using the format of Jacqui Schiff from *Cathexis Reader* with some modifications, we might conceptualize discounting in the following way.

LEVEL	AREA		
	Feelings	*Problem*	*Option*
Existence	Presence of feelings	Presence of a problem(s)	Presence of an option(s)
Significance	Importance of feelings	Importance of a problem(s)	Importance of an option(s)

Possibility of *Change*	Possibility of changing feeling(s)	Possibility of solving problem(s)	Possibility of using options(s)
Personal *Ability*	To change feeling(s)	To solve the problem(s)	To use the option(s)

Some examples of discounts at each level of feelings might be:

> *Existence:* "You're not angry; you're just tired!"
> *Significance*: "Of course you're angry, but that isn't important now!"
> *Possibility of Change:* "I have to be angry; there's no other way to feel!"
> *Personal Ability:* "I, for one, am not able to 'grin and bear it.' "

Examples at each level of problems are:

> *Existence:* "You may see a problem here, but I certainly don't."
> *Significance:* "Of course there's a problem, but it's not important."
> *Possibility of Change:* "He'll always create a problem; that's just him!"
> *Personal Ability:* "I'm never able to deal with a problem like this."

In the area of options some examples could be:

> *Existence:* "There are no options; You're married and stuck!"
> *Significance:* "I could run away or continue to try to work this out, but those things wouldn't mean anything to her. Things have gone too far!"
> *Possibility of Change:* "Even if I went back to college and got a good job things would still be the same."
> *Personal Ability:* "Others might separate or get divorced, but I could never do those things."

As indicated above, some of these statements might not be a "put-down." Maybe I *am* tired and not angry, maybe "he" will always be a trouble-maker, etc. They are discounts when said without reasonable reflection or consideration.

How do we handle discounting in ourselves and in others? The first step is to stop rewarding them with laughter. Silence short-circuits the discount cycle. It says that discounts are not acceptable here. Support from others is desirable with this approach, since it may anger the discounter who responds with more insults: "Where's your sense of humor?" "Get out of the wrong side of the bed this morning?" "Man, he's a sourpuss!" If there are others around who also do not laugh this kind of retaliation is less likely.

If we ourselves have the habit of discounting others or the situation, we need to become more aware of our style of relating to and communicating with others. We need to try a different style: be positive, be complimentary when appropriate and retire from the stage. Stop trying to get laughs. You'll feel more relaxed. To make the first step in this direction we need to be convinced that discounting poisons the environment and puts distance between ourselves and others.

Also, we need to have a healthy self-image, a conviction that we are useful, productive, valuable persons in ourselves. We do not need to put others down so that we can appear "up." We do not allow others to put us down so that they can feel up either, not even "bosses." Of course, we'll slip now and again, feeling that a "zinger" is just too good to miss or simply forgetting. Practice and perseverance will pay off with renewed tranquillity and the personal satisfaction of feeling coherent and purposeful. We'll find that we also stop discounting ourselves.

To stop others from discounting, some form of confrontation may be necessary. This may best be done in private, but public confrontation is appropriate if the "busting" persists. A brief format for confronting recommended by some students of human behavior has three steps: (1) describe the offending statement (or event), (2) describe its feeling impact on yourself, and (3) describe the behavioral consequences for yourself as a result of your feelings. For example: "John, when you say that I did not write that report I delivered this morning, even in 'kidding,' it makes me feel angry and upset, so that I can't concentrate on what I'm doing. It takes me a while to settle down."

The primary intended effect of this approach is to convey to the other that while he or she is involved, the problem is one's own. We do not intend to put the other "on the spot" or to point a finger of blame. Our intent is to share with him or her the effects of his or her behavior. We do not make judgments about the behavior of the other, except to share with him or her the effect such behavior has on us personally.

It is most important that the discounter recall the statement that upset us. If they do not recall it, forget the confrontation. They will leave muttering: "He said I said that, but I don't think I did. He misunderstood!" and no learning will take place.

While discounting, in my experience, is the major occasion for difficulty among co-workers, it is not the only culprit. Several other personality conflicts, relationship habits and interpersonal factors can also occasion difficult people. I have discussed many of these in the first three chapters of this book.

SURVIVAL STRATEGIES

1. Never use "discounts." I know that *never* is used only by God. In this case, we need to share with God. Never means never.
2. Don't support discounts with laughter. Let them sink into silence.
3. Refuse to be discounted. Share your discomfort with the discounter in private. If that doesn't stop the discounter, share your non-approval in the company of others. Be assertive and balanced: "When you said . . . I felt foolish and it took me ten minutes to settle down. Please don't do that again." We may change the wording to fit our style, but it always needs to be assertive and ADULT.

Before we conclude this discussion, however, we need to consider one dynamic that rivals discounting in the world of work. Discounting, in fact, may only be a tool of this dynamic. It is the choice that most of us have to make between being competitive and being cooperative. These are attitudes that can strongly influence the world in which we work. Certainly, we need to be competitive with other organizations and companies that compete with our products. That is not a problem. That is business. However, when we are needlessly competitive within our own company, we can create difficult people or be difficult people.

Ordinarily competition finds more difficult people than does cooperation. Sometimes competition is appropriate, such as between similar businesses, in a contest or in striving for promotions. Even though appropriate, however, competition is the soil in which difficult people grow. Hostility builds, we view "our" side only positively and the other side as only negative, members of either side accept even dictatorial leadership for the sake of unity, compromise is seen as treason and concessions are perceived as "sell-outs." It is a mix filled with potential for difficult people.

In our work world, competition and cooperation are often a matter of perception and attitude. Rarely do we consider which is most appropriate. Our different perceptions may be outlined as follows.

Competitive Approach	*Cooperative Approach*
1. We pursue our *own* goals	1. We pursue goals *held in common*
2. secrecy is valued	2. openness is valued
3. we don't let others know what we really want	3. we accurately describe what we really want to others
4. we use strategies that are unpredictable and utilize the element of surprise	4. we do not try to surprise others, but we can be flexible
5. threats and bluffs are acceptable	5. threats and bluffs are not used
6. we *appear* to be committed to a position; logical and illogical arguments are acceptable for this purpose	6. we try to find solutions to problems with logical and innovative processes

Competitive Approach	*Cooperative Approach*
7. we form bad stereotypes of the other side, ignoring their logic and we escalate hostility	7. we refuse to accept stereotypes of any kind, insist that ideas be considered on their own merit and endeavor to avoid deliberate hostility
8. PATHOLOGICAL EXTREME: everything that impedes the other's goal must facilitate the accomplishment of our goal	8. PATHOLOGICAL EXTREME: whatever is good for others and for the group is good for oneself; will not take responsibility for self

We need to be able to compete when it is appropriate. We need to recognize those situations when cooperation is appropriate. The win-lose dynamic of competition makes people difficult and we should expect that. Cooperation decreases the likelihood of difficult people. Our problem lies in the different perceptions people have about the same situation, some viewing it as competitive, others viewing it as cooperative.

Co-workers expect *some* competition. Neither we nor they expect those behaviors described above that can be seriously destructive to ourselves or others. If "they" do expect this kind of behavior, they need to be avoided. The destructive people should be left to themselves. We are not the saviors of the world. If we need to deal with them, we do so "from a distance."

Chances are that we do need to deal with such inappropriately competitive individuals on occasion. Keep in mind the following when that is necessary:

1. Keep your own goals and objectives in mind; don't be diverted.
2. Don't withdraw; keep the channels of communication open, even in the face of discount or insult; use the methods suggested above when useful.
3. Don't use inflammatory or emotional words; stay "Adult" as described in Chapter 2.
4. Listen; support constructive criticism.

5. Allow others to be wrong on occasion, to come to their own conclusions and to change their minds without feelings like "sell-outs."
6. Use sound structures for problem solving and decision making.

In the world of business, competition is common. We need not be disturbed by it; we do need to know how to handle it when it enters our lives. It need not be destructive.

Summary

Work difficulties occupy a good piece of our lives. They may be occasioned by the job itself, by the style of management we experience or by our co-workers. Quality Circles can help, but they might not have reached our region yet. Perhaps we need to introduce them.

To be satisfying our job needs to be as complete as possible; we need to have maximum control over it and receive significant feedback on it. Not all of these conditions can be fulfilled all of the time, but we need to try for most of them.

Management styles can create difficulties. It helps if we recognize them as the source of problems on occasion. We do not keep blaming ourselves. Developmental management rarely creates problems; if it does, they are real problems that call for creative solutions. Controlling, relinquishing and defensive management progressively create difficulties that employees are ill-equipped to handle. It is helpful simply to recognize them as the occasion of the difficulty. Sometimes, ambiguity about the source of a problem, as we shall see in the next chapter, can be more frustrating than the inability to solve the problem.

But it is not always the fault of the system. Fellow workers create difficulties. Workers can be their own worst enemies. They "bust," "put down" or discount each other to make work life miserable. Legitimate competition can mask the need for needed cooperation. The "good guys" need to keep their balance, to confront discounts when required, to ignore them when useful, to recognize unproductive competition and to frustrate its illicit direction.

Most of the difficulties we experience and accept in the world of work are allowed to continue because of our own co-operation and/or stupidity. We can create our own environment of "no discounts" and "appropriate cooperation" if we use the techniques suggested in this chapter. We need only the courage to be different, a difference that, for the most part, will be welcomed by all.

Intelligence and knowledge are fine, but feelings rule the world, even the work world. They influence the way jobs are constructed and the way managers and co-workers relate. We need to reflect on handling feelings next.

6

Feelings and Difficulties

Feelings are sometimes like hot potatoes in our hands. All of us have feelings. All of us probably have, at some time in our life, had a hot potato or two in our hands. Sometimes like hot potatoes we have asked ourselves about feelings: "What do we do with them? Where do we put them?" At other times we know just what to do with feelings like happiness, contentment, comfort and joy. We hug them and enjoy them. Since this is a book about difficult people and difficult situations we shall deal with only "hot potatoes" in this chapter. Nice feelings do not usually accompany difficulty.

Nita is a friend of mine who, like most of us, has had to learn where to put hot potatoes. A year ago she called me on the phone one evening "just to talk." It turned out that she had been a victim of a game her new boss played on her that day. In the morning he had told her to make use of his secretary when she had need, since his need of the secretary would be minimal for the next few weeks. He was traveling and doing work only he could do. In the afternoon Nita had given work to her boss' secretary and was shortly called to his office. The boss said: "I said try to keep the secretary busy. Don't inundate her. I need her help too, you know. Use your head."

Nita knew that she flushed; she stammered "I'm sorry" and hastily retreated, confused and disturbed. She didn't know how she felt, and still didn't know that evening. Was she sorry, angry or resentful? And how could she handle any of these feelings even if she could identify them? She had eaten little at dinner and "just knew" she wouldn't be able to sleep that night.

Knowing something can often be almost pure brain activity. Feeling something generally engages the whole self, mind and body. Nita was mentally confused, physically flushed, without appetite and "wound up." Over eight hundred years ago a famous philosopher and theologian, Thomas Aquinas, defined feelings as "movements of the sensory appetites," such as anger over being wronged or exhilaration over being successful. One psychologist, R.E. Brennan, paraphrased Aquinas' definition as: "Emotions are movements of the sensory appetites, following upon recognition of some stimulus, and characterized by definite modifications in the regulated activities of the body." Feelings are so total that the body itself registers their presence. As we shall see below, there is no such thing as not expressing feelings. They *will be expressed*, appropriately or inappropriately (cf. *General Psychology*, Macmillan, N.Y., 1937, p. 264).

In general, most psychologists agree that we at least need to acknowledge our feelings, to "own" them, if we are to remain mentally healthy. But, then, several questions arise: How can we utilize feelings to move toward desired goals? How can we avoid allowing feelings to become destructive, to ourselves as well as to others? How much do we need to know about the sources of our feelings? Do all of us need to search our childhood experiences to understand our feelings? What are some ways we can handle our feelings and deal with the feelings of others in a constructive context? These are the questions we shall respond to in this chapter.

Recognizing Our Feelings

In the early part of my training in process education I was acting as a trainer for a small committee in our township. As I observed the group, it became clearer and clearer that two particular members had teamed up against Emma, a new committee member. One or the other regularly contradicted or disagreed with anything Emma said. Emma flushed a bit at the first rebuttals and eventually pushed her chair back a little from the table. Eventually she fell silent.

I felt that a good deal of learning could come out of Emma's behavior and the transactions between her and the two opposing committee members, so I focused on this segment of the meeting in the feedback session. Emma admitted that she knew she was regularly being refuted by the same people. I asked her: "How did you feel about that?" "Nothing" was her reply. Perhaps because I was new to training technique or perhaps because Emma regularly denied her feelings, I could not discover whether Emma was angry or not. She seemed to be from the flushes and her behavior of pushing her chair back and being silent. She seemed to choose to express her anger, if it was there, non-verbally, if she made a conscious choice at all.

We cannot not feel. It is part of the animal and human dimensions of our make-up. Difficulties arise from negating our feelings, mostly because they surface one way or the other and, if left to themselves without cognitive guidance, they usually surface with poor effect.

On the other hand, we need not *act* on every feeling we have. A child acts out his or her feelings and needs to be taught that he or she has a choice to act on a feeling or not. He or she is taught that anger and resentment are legitimate feelings and it is healthy to own our feelings, but he or she can choose not to act on every feeling he or she has. He or she can acknowledge the feeling, even share it with the person whose behavior aroused the feeling, but he or she can then walk away from that feeling. Punching some other child or adult is not always the necessary consequence of feeling anger. There are other outlets. Sometimes the difficult person has not learned that there is such a choice.

Bob, a dear friend of mine, remains my friend because I avoid him when he is angry. He has an awesome temper and has found himself involved in many a barroom ruckus. For Bob to be angry is to punch something or someone. Once he broke a knuckle hitting a concrete wall. We've discussed his problem when he brought it up, but he can't see that he has any choice but action when he feels anger. "Talkin' or walkin' don't do the job," he says.

It might help "to do our job" of recognizing feelings and of responding constructively to them if we reflect for a few moments on those parts of the personality that give rise to feelings. In Chapter 4 we described the use Transactional Analysis makes of *Parent* and *Child*, as well as *Adult*, in attempting to help us understand our behavioral patterns. Further elaboration on these states of personality will help to throw more light on the sources of our feelings.

Both Parent and Child personality states possess feelings. The Parent may have compassion, caring, love, resentment, fear or anger according to the professionals. As a result the Parent may be nurturing or critical. The Child may feel joy, love, conceit, hatred or resentment, depending on whether it is the Natural Child or the Adapted Child (that state formed early in life to adapt to outside pressures) that has precedence at a given moment. Both Parent and Child can cover the range of emotions.

The Adult has no feelings of itself. It can energize the Parent or the Child to feel and to express emotion as the Adult thinks appropriate. The Adult can know when feeling is appropriate, in other words, but it must call on Parent or Child to do the feeling.

Individuals with integrated personalities are rarely difficult people. An integrated personality is one in which the Adult is the executor, utilizing the Parent and/or the Child as the Adult deems appropriate. Knowing ourselves partially involves knowing why we feel as we do, particularly when we have bad feelings, since these regularly cause difficulty for ourselves and others. Knowing others sometimes includes making educated guesses about the reasons for their behavior and feelings. We can never be sure, of course, about the inner dynamics of another, but it sometimes helps us to have *possible* reasons for the actions of others.

Ray Novaco of the University of California at Irvine calls this process of coming up with possible reasons for the behavior of others the "reappraisal method." He suspects that our feelings, such as anger, resentment, etc., are maintained or even enhanced by the remarks we make to ourselves or to others when we become angry, etc., such as "What a nerve she has!" or "Who does he think he is?" So, he teaches his students to reappraise the situation by suggesting less inflammatory reasons for difficult behavior: "She must be feeling poorly today," or "Maybe something got him upset." The Adult calls on the Parent or Child for reasons that might excuse the difficult behavior. Such a method can reduce the difficulty we experience with others, since it seems that the more we concentrate on a single emotion, such as anger or resentment, the stronger it becomes. And the more we can excuse it, the less upset we are (cf. C. Tavris, "Anger Defused," *Psychology Today,* November 1982, pp. 32 and 35).

We experience difficulty when the Parent or Child feels outside of the awareness of the Adult. Edna, a school teacher, for instance, could never become angry. When it would be appropriate for her to have been angry, she always became sad. Her life, as a result, was not often happy. She did not have good class discipline, accepted unjustified poor performance appraisals from supervisors and principals without comment and never fought with her chauvinist husband. While attending a self-help workshop Edna came upon a startling insight: throughout her childhood no one in her family was permitted to be angry; anger was not acceptable in her house. Since she had to feel "something" when wronged, her Child chose to feel sad, unbeknown to her Adult until that workshop. She had found herself difficult and others found it difficult to reach her because her Child was "doing its own thing" outside of her Adult awareness.

Feelings are as varied as life itself and just as complex, so it is not likely that we could have a formula that would enable us to identify the infallible source of each of our feelings. But there are some clues that might indicate that our Parent or Child is doing our feeling for us without our Adult being aware of what is happening.

Parent domination might be indicated by habitual depression, negativism, feeling responsible for people or events outside of our possible control, feeling frustrated when we are not in full control, nurturing when and/or where it is not useful or is even harmful, feeling a need to judge and evaluate everything, feeling patronizing to others while not recognizing their talents or feeling consistent disappointment with others.

Child domination might be indicated by habitual anger, resentment or hostility, by a pervasive fear of doing wrong, making errors or of being corrected, by a constant need to please everyone and feelings of failure when others are not pleased, by feeling a need to be deceitful, dishonest or "clever," by arrogant feelings, persistent feelings of conceit, stubbornness and self-centeredness and by constant feelings of jealousy.

There are, of course, good, healthy feelings in both the Parent and the Child, feelings of caring in the Parent and of joy and love in the Child. We are focusing on the trouble-makers here because we are trying to understand better those feelings that create or result from difficulty.

Since all of us feel and since, as suggested, feelings that go unrecognized and are not accepted by the feeler can cause difficulty for the feeler as well as for others, there is a good deal of value in each of us reflecting on what part our own Parent and Child play in our feelings. We need to consider whether they are acting on their own and when they are acting on their own without the awareness of the Adult. The Adult, then, has no opportunity to consider the appropriateness of feelings of which it is not aware. In other words, we need to bring cognition and reason into the experience of feeling. Reason needs to be able to ask whether this or that feeling will accomplish our goals effectively if expressed appropriately. Every feeling is expressed in some way, but anger, for instance, need not always be expressed by a catharsis, an uproar or even by quiet conversation. On the other hand, our feelings might best be expressed to achieve our goals. Much depends on the circumstances surrounding the feeling. We hinted this above. Now we shall think about it in more detail.

SURVIVAL STRATEGIES

1. Acknowledge your own feelings. You don't have to act on them, but you need to accept ownership of them. Only then can you choose to act on them or not.

2. Rather than attributing "bad" motivations to difficult persons, consider less inflammatory reasons they might have for acting difficult, e.g., maybe they are in physical pain or there might be a family problem. Our own disturbance is less likely to feed on the suspected "nastiness" of another.

3. Work at recognizing consistent feeling patterns in yourself. See if you can trace these patterns to your Parent or Child ego states. If you can, bring your Adult in to examine the patterns: "Are they reasonable? Appropriate?" If you decide that the patterns are illogical leftovers from earlier situations and behaviors, work toward changing them by forcing yourself *to think* when the patterns begin to be active, by doing some difficult arithmetic that requires you *to think* or by trying to recite the Gettysburg Address. When your Adult is active, examine the feeling pattern and look at ways you can interrupt and change the pattern, if you want to do so.

How, When, and "If" To Express Feelings

Brian was angry. He had had another long and loud argument with his wife. Angrily he slammed the door to his house as he headed for his favorite bar where he could find friends. Having found them Brian poured out his tale of unjust treatment, ingratitude, etc., to receive consolation and support. He didn't get over his anger, even though he "let it all hang out." In fact, through no fault of the beer, he got more angry. He focused more accurately on his grievances, clasped them more securely to his cause and found himself practicing for the inevitable encounter upon his return home.

Perhaps Brain did not pick the best spot or the best persons to ventilate his feelings, but in the light of recent studies it seems that Brian's experience is fairly universal. The common wisdom of "talking out our feelings" is being seriously questioned. It seems that for many of us talking about our anger, depression, resentment, fear, etc., can make those feelings more intense and more difficult to deal with. Even if we don't "talk out loud," mulling over feelings of anger, resentment, etc., tends to reinforce them. In short, if we want to get rid of bad feelings, it seems best to seek activities and interests that will distract us from them.

There are some reasons for this intensity following our attempts at catharsis. One is that catharsis assumes that there is a single, identifiable feeling of which we need to be rid. Usually, however, recent studies have indicated that there are few uncontaminated feelings. Anger, fear and resentment often travel together. Rage and sadness are often companions. Attempts at a catharsis often lead us to isolate one feeling and to concentrate on it, making that feeling more intense while excluding the associated feelings. Our "catharsis" convinces us that we really are angry or resentful or fearful with a passion. Identifying the feelings encourages us to repeat our reasons for feeling so, with the result that we maintain and enhance the feeling.

Carol Tavris, in the article mentioned above, reports on one study in which employees who lost their jobs when their plant closed were interviewed. Some were asked questions such as "Could your supervisor(s) have done anything to keep the plant open?" and "Was management in any way responsible for the closing of the plant?" Most of the employees so questioned became more hostile toward those whom they felt could have saved their jobs as a result of discussing such questions. They were more willing to speak of their anger against those individuals they blamed, even in public, following the interviews. Only if an employee blamed himself or herself for their loss did this hostility become less with time.

Another reason that attempts at catharsis might backfire is that feelings generally are expressed within a particular situation and to certain individuals. Only when we rehearse the feeling in our own head is this not true. An aggressive release of anger may bring sharp retorts from another, resulting in an emotional build-up and a brouhaha, depending on who the "other" is. Or it may bring relief, if we have judged the other correctly as understanding and supportive. Even the low-keyed, psychologically suggested method of confronting the other with "When you do such-and-such, I feel resentful, and as a result I cannot (do my work) (concentrate)" may have re-verse effect if the other does not respond to our confrontation. There are some difficult people who are moved only by an up-roar. In this context we have to scream to find relief, if we need to move them. If we don't need to do so, distracting our-selves is still the better method for getting rid of bad feelings. One point is that there is a time and place to express our feel-ings if that is necessary to achieve our goal. Another point is that we simmer down more quickly if we don't have to contin-ue dealing with bad feelings.

SURVIVAL STRATEGIES

1. If you don't want disturbing feelings to intensify, distract yourself by concentrating on things not related to the feel-ings.
2. Sometimes, but not often (hopefully), an individual only hears us if we get angry. If it is important to us that the per-son hear us, express anger, knowing what we are doing and keeping ourselves under control. If we can smile to our-selves and say "That ought to do it" after the uproar, we have expressed controlled anger appropriately for a pur-pose.

A Syndrome of Bad Feelings and Difficult People

We have reflected that feelings do not live in isolation. The world of feelings is very complex, existing, as they do, in the whole person and even within the social relationships between persons. A feeling rarely exists in a "pure" state. Usually it is entangled with other feelings. When we consider feelings and difficult people, feelings always live in our relationships. Still, we can uncover a kind of syndrome or system, a set of components, that underlie the birth, growth, experience and expression of bad feelings in difficult people. In this sense we are going to isolate bad feelings in difficult people for our better understanding. As indicated in the beginning of this book, better understanding often leads to greater tolerance and even appreciation of behavior that is disturbing and destructive if left in ignorance.

I suggest that there are two classes of bad feelings. One class arises out of frustration and includes anger, resentment and depression (sadness and despair). The other class arises from feeling inadequate and includes fear, anxiety and guilt. All of these feelings can be legitimate, given a reasonable stimulus and situation. It is very reasonable, for instance, to feel depressed when one has lost a job in mid-life, or to feel anger when wrongly accused or to feel fear when attacked by a mugger. They become an unhealthy syndrome in difficult people when they are felt without a reasonable stimulus and/or outside of a reasonable situation. They become seriously unhealthy when they become an habitual attitude.

These two classes of feelings can overlap in the same individual. The same person may have some feelings of frustration as well as of inadequacy. For the sake of illustration, however, I've chosen Lori and Frank. Lori illustrated the creation of a difficult person out of frustration. Frank was a classic example of how feelings of inadequacy can make a person difficult.

Lori was a successful lawyer, passing her bar examination at the age of twenty-four and practicing law with a highly regarded law firm for six years. She then married and conceded to the wishes of her husband that she leave her career and be a full-time wife and mother (when children came). The prospect appealed to Lori, probably because she loved her husband deeply. Children came quickly and after five years Lori found herself indeed a full-time wife and mother, but she also found some resentment in herself. As she thought about her brief career and her talents, reliving the pleasure she derived from the practice of law, and as she watched the satisfaction her husband found in his job, she became more resentful and angry. Of course, in time she became depressed, making life difficult for her husband as well as her children. She became a "nag" and a fault finder. Frustration was making Lori difficult.

Frank was a high school teacher who decided to establish a small business just before the recession of the late 1970's and early 1980's. At first the business did well, but with the continuing recession it crumbled, like so many other small businesses. Because teachers were not in great demand, Frank was unable to find a job in his profession. He was forced to take unpleasant jobs that paid little. He was feeling inadequate, even developing sexual impotency. He feared that he would never attain the position or satisfaction he had enjoyed as a teacher, and he felt guilty for "destroying" his own life and risking the welfare of his family. As his business had failed, he became more belligerent toward his employees, making cutting remarks and belittling them. He brought this attitude home with him and became a difficult person for his wife and children. He could not give them financial security and felt insecure enough not to be able to give them peace and tranquillity. Feelings of inadequacy made Frank a difficult person.

Should you have to deal with Lori or Frank, or with people who have built themselves up to be difficult, you not only have to deal with yourself but with them as well. You need to deal not only with your own mounting anger and resentment, but with the inner dynamics of Loris and Franks. The complexity of the feeling situation should now be clear. Relationships and feelings are usually inseparable. You could be the target of their hostility. So, what do you do?

To deal with Loris and Franks we need to be aware of various behaviors that indicate the syndrome of the difficult person. Such behaviors are part of the syndrome:

1. A person may lie in wait. All goes well until another behaves in unacceptable ways, even though the other acts unconsciously. Loris and Franks attack with ferocity, accusing the

violator of betraying their trust and rejecting the other (you) immediately.

2. Some Loris and Franks are habitually angry, regularly critiquing others for failing to live up to their expectations; they respond negatively and with bitterness as a matter of course.

3. Other difficult people such as Lori and Frank live in a pervasive world of persecution. "Others" are aiming to belittle or destroy them. Lori and Frank need to be on guard at all times. They are justified in attacking and destroying their opponents at any time.

Harry Levinson, the author of *Emotional Health: In the World of Work*, suggests that a common theme or attitude among difficult people who use hostility "is the inability to trust others and the effort to suppress the hurtful actions of others. A parallel theme is the extreme difficulty in accepting the possibility that one may be wrong. Together these traits make for a guarded readiness to defend and attack" (Harper and Row, N.Y. 1964, p. 96). In essence, Levinson suggests that difficult people are made so by distrust, suppression of hurts and a dominant conviction of righteousness.

When a person does lose control over his aggression, there *are* ways to diffuse the hostile situation:

(1) Absorb the hostility, refusing to become hostile or angry yourself, so that the other need not escalate his or her hostility.

(2) Permit the other to be angry and to lose control, as long as others are not hurt. Do not withdraw or become angry in return, so that the other sees that you recognize that anger and hostility are possibly appropriate. This is principally accomplished by your own calm attitude. It says that you understand why the other is upset.

(3) Do not support the repetition of the hostile behavior; let the other know that while you understand his reaction in this instance, it is not acceptable to act this way in the future. There are other ways to diffuse the stress and to make one's point (cf. Levinson, *op. cit.*, p. 101).

SURVIVAL STRATEGIES

1. Ordinarily, don't meet hostility with hostility nor anger with anger. The difficulty can be handled more easily if we don't allow it to escalate.
2. Accept the expression of anger or hostility as *sometimes* appropriate, but not always. Show this by calm behavior in the face of anger/hostility. If it is important enough and if your relationship with the other is sound, you may find it useful to talk with the other about different ways to handle a difficulty, when feelings have settled down.

The syndrome of the hostile feelings of difficult people has been up-front and obvious in our discussion. Often this is reality—but not always. Difficult people can be subtle without intending or even recognizing their own subtlety. We can be left whirling after a discussion with a difficult person, feeling unfulfilled, confused and disoriented. Neither we nor the other might be able to explain why.

One explanation might be the mechanism of "redefinition," a process used consciously or unconsciously by another to maintain his or her own frame of reference. Everything you communicate is "redefined" by the other, so that it fits into his or her own field of knowledge, experience or competence.

An example: you have spoken to Lenny about a new territory the boss has asked you to open. It seems filled with possibilities. You are enthusiastic. Your respect for Lenny has been long and public. You have "backed him up" time after time. To you he is a kind of patriarch. You describe the opportunity to Lenny: "It's a whole new field. The opposition has not even touched the area. You know that there is a need for your product, for our product here." Lenny replies, "Yeah. I know the feeling. Once I had an opportunity to go to Europe and to search out new resources for the company. It was a great trip. I enjoyed it, and I established a lot of contacts. When I was in Naples . . ." So Lenny continues. He does not speak to your opportunity. He redefines the issue in the light of his own experience. Lenny is a difficult person, with a great deal of unintended subtlety. He needs to meet his own needs, and he does it, often, at our expense. But it is unintentional, expecially if Lenny is an older man or woman. We do tend to look back, rather than forward.

Another example: Betty is a dress buyer. After a trip to New York she is convinced that suits for women are in fashion for spring. Her supervisor responds, "Well, I'm most interested. Five years ago I suggested that casual wear was the fashion of the year. It made sense. During the era of Johnson and Kennedy people wanted to look casual. I had great success with the line, and it might very well come back again. Golly, I enjoyed those days." The point is that the supervisor has redefined the conversation. He or she has given no response to Betty's decision, for which Betty sought support. The supervisor has become a difficult person.

Redefinition is a process by which individuals maintain a frame of reference in which they are comfortable. Anyone can find himself or herself using it. We want to maintain an established view of ourselves, of other people and/or of the world. Being unwilling to accept new and different concepts that may occasion new and different perspectives, we take what another says and reinterpret it so that we can deal with it, so that we can speak to it within our comfortable and experienced frame of reference. Without realizing or intending it, we become difficult people because others cannot communicate with us. They speak of their own needs and we reflect on our experiences that have no or little relationship to the present (cf. J. Schiff, *Cathexis Reader,* Harper & Row, N.Y., 1975, pp. 54–68).

It is generally risky to pinpoint the *cause* of a behavior. From experience and theory, however, I choose to take that risk: feelings are the cause of redefinition. People need the kind of affirmation that comes from placing reality within a comfortable context. Most of the time "redefiners" are asking for help and support.

We can give that support by realigning our conversation and interest toward their interests. This is a kind of "stroking" or support that says "You are important." It brings solace to the other. It also usually leads to a dead end, the monologue of the other concluding the conversation with little or no satisfaction on the part of either discussant. The "other" senses that the point has been missed, but is willing to let it pass. You know it has been missed and feel small comfort in your effort to alleviate the pain of the other. You need to look elsewhere for a "sounding board."

We can handle redefinition, as we can handle most problems, by avoiding the people who redefine. Whether we do this or not depends on our sense of values and priorities. Usually redefiners need us. We can choose to be patient and to wait out their conscious sensibilities, which are not in any way guaranteed, with the hope that having an audience will help the redefiner. It generally does not help. It often intensifies his or her redefinition. Perhaps the kindest thing we can do is to avoid the redefiner, with the hope that he or she will recognize the problem.

We can confront the redefiner, but there is little hope of success in this approach. Redefiners are in their own world. This is particularly true if the redefiner is facing serious problems, or even death, without our understanding or knowledge.

Bill was my father-in-law. During October a few years ago I had occasion to stay with him while attending a workshop in his area. He lived alone. Bill and I had been close. I was now almost unemployed. Bill had been my confidant for six or seven years. We had two or three evenings together, at the close of each day's workshop. Each evening I would begin to speak to him about my concerns and fears. Each evening he would turn those concerns and fears around to his own experiences of the past.

"Bill, I'm not sure how long this job at the college is going to last. I have some consultant jobs, but I'm not sure how far they can take me."

"Yeah," said Bill. "You know, I really enjoyed my time with Mary in Scotland. That was a trip I'll never forget. There was one little town, typically Scottish, that had the best Scotch I've tasted. It was almost like that twenty-five-year-old we tasted at the Tesper Club."

"You really enjoyed that trip, didn't you, Bill?" I said, in an effort to maintain communication.

"It was the best," said Bill as he went to make himself a drink.

"The workshop today was interesting," I said, as Bill returned.

"Yeah! I guess it was," he said. "My work is really getting difficult these days. They want me on the road and yet they want me in the store. I almost had it out with the boss the other day."

And so the conversation progressed for a three hour evening. I left the next morning in confusion, feeling I had lost a friend but not knowing how or why. Two months later I found that Bill had cancer, had known he had it the night we spent together. Looking back I see his redefinition as a desperate cry for support, interest and affirmation. The "difficult person" now seemed less difficult to understand. Bill was living with the knowledge of his own death. I was concerned about the intricacies of my life.

I am sure there are ways to work with redefinition. Jacqui Schiff discusses some ways in her book, *Cathexis Reader,* already cited. But Jacqui deals with psychotics. We need to deal with those who are not mentally ill but who use techniques that avoid communication and create difficulties. We can do the following:

1. Assume that the redefiner is in serious need of support and try to give it. Enough support can lead the redefiner into reality or it can deepen the sense of isolation.

2. Avoid the redefiner, particularly if we feel we cannot help.

3. Confront the redefiner. If redefinition continues, recognize the need for professional help of a medical or psychological nature and, if you have the energy, stay with him or her.

In short, there is no easy way of handling the redefiner as a difficult person. Usually, however, they need our help more than our criticism.

Another Feeling Design of Difficult People

There is another fatal process used by difficult people to attain their purposes. It is fatal because it is death-dealing to themselves (sometimes even physically) and to others (at least psychologically). But it is unconscious. It is a learned behavior that allows the person to achieve recognition, attention and personal satisfaction. It is called a *racket* in the literature of Transactional Analysis: an unconscious design to use inappropriate feelings to achieve needed fulfillment goals of attention and, therefore, of survival.

A word is needed about the importance of recognition and attention. As children we need to be physically stroked, coddled and touched. Some studies indicate that without such experiences children physically die. As we grow older, those physical needs are translated into psychological needs: the need for acknowledgement of our existence, of our value and/or of our competence. We have a desperate physical and psychological need to be acknowledged by others.

A racket is a distorted design, engineered by the individual in the light of earlier experience, to get such recognition.

Kathy is a superb electronic analyst. She is able to "trouble-shoot" any electronic instrument from televisions to computers. She is highly valued in her firm. But Kathy is not easy to deal with. Ever since she came to the firm she has belittled her own competence, having to be persuaded to handle job after job. She is always "uncertain," "not sure of what is needed," or "unfulfilled by success." She is a *pain* before and after the repair job.

In spite of Kathy's competence, she has long been programmed to feel incompetent. She found early in life that she attracted more attention when she was "weak" than when she was "strong." Unconsciously, she uses this *racket* to acquire the attention she needs for survival.

It may have begun long ago during a fire in her home, when she was too small to be of help. She was caught up by her parents in the midst of the flames, rushed outside and showered with kisses. Or it may have been generated by her position in a family of ten as the youngest. She was not expected to be able in most activities. She received attention when she was the weakest, the most vulnerable, the least able. So Kathy unconsciously developed a racket: an unconscious design to use feelings of incompetence to receive attention. Kathy is an unknown to herself; to others, she is a difficult person, one with a great deal of talent who needs always to be persuaded to use it. In the eyes of some she is a "prima donna."

How to deal with Kathy(s)? There is no short process, no short-cut. She needs to be reprogrammed, to learn that there are rewards for being readily competent and able. She needs lots of compliments for ready competence and to be ignored when she professes inability. Others need to be brought in to fill the need she could have met, if she had acted. If her condition persists, she may have to be separated from her job with professional help suggested. As in the cases of redefinition, there are no ready or easy solutions. Some difficult people cannot be helped except by professionals.

The psychological phenomenon of "projection" can be a classical example of a racket. A person has been raised to reject anger as a legitimate response in most aggravating situations. Within a Christian context, they may have been taught to "love their enemies," to the exclusion of just anger. However, while it was not consistent with such teaching, they learned that they may be angry with those who are hostile to them. Their final interpretation has been that they can be hostile to others as long as they are convinced that others are hostile to them.

Steve is a shipping clerk in a large department store. Usually his job is uneventful and predictable. But Steve has a lot of hostility in himself, resentful that he has been a shipping clerk for so many years, passed over time and time again for promotion. He comes from a good family, one that did not accept anger or resentment in the home. However, if anyone attacked the family, all kinds of hostility was voiced, planned and acted upon. Steve was taught to attack his enemy, as long as it was not family. There were no prohibitions against provoking others, and, once they were hostile, it was permissible to react angrily against them. Steve has used this tactic recently, attempting to relieve his own hostile feelings related to non-promotion and non-recognition, by attacking others. He has projected his own hostility on others to give himself permission to be hostile. He has become a difficult person.

Steve can be helped by a good friend who is able to convince him that he is his own worst enemy, that others are not "out to get him." He is fundamentally scared. He is afraid of being ignored, passed over and belittled. A close friend can allay such concerns. If, of course, Steve's concerns have become a serious issue, a kind of paranoia, he needs professional help. But this is not ordinarily needed where the background influence is as superficial as described. Usually, support, camaraderie and friendship can short circuit unjustified feelings of hostility. When we are wanted by others, hostility is not needed (cf. Levinson, *op. cit.*, p. 106). All of us need a place in the world, a place where we are appreciated.

SURVIVAL STRATEGIES

Rackets are often as much of a problem to the person afflicted with them as to others. To maintain your own tranquillity *ignore* the other's rackety behavior and *support* non-racket behavior. This will also help the person with the racket, since he or she may drop a racket that is no longer bringing any rewards or recognition. But don't expect quick change. Just consistently support non-racket behavior.

Ways To Handle Feelings

It seems that there is no one sure way to handle the variety of feelings that are experienced by the difficult person. Feelings of anger, resentment and depression that arise from frustration can be met in many, many different ways. Feelings of fear, anxiety and guilt that issue from feelings of inadequacy or impotence have no one panacea. The complexity of human feelings does not allow for simple solutions.

We can develop some general approaches. Stephen Karpman, M.D. suggests that there are four criteria that must be met if we are to handle feelings in difficult people (cf. "Options," *Transactional Analysis Journal,* January 1971, pp. 79–87). I shall not adhere to Dr. Karpman's criteria in detail, but I do acknowledge his article as igniting my own suggestions.

If we are to handle *most feelings* in others that create difficulty for us we need to (1) change our approach/attitude, (2) respond in a way that is not expected, (3) change the subject so that the difficult area of discussion is put aside. I have combined two of Dr. Karpman's criteria.

We need to change our approach/attitude. Difficult people may say things that are intended to make us feel impotent, weak or dependent. We need to reject that original feeling, accepting it as a fully natural reaction to dominating or parental comments, and to adopt our own independent response.

Barbara is a secretary in a medical office. She is at the call of three doctors. One of the physicians is regularly critical of Barbara. Such remarks as "Can't you get *anything* right?" or "You can't seem to meet our standards around here" are common. Barbara's first reaction is one of fear and anxiety, reminiscent of the way she felt when her mother or father corrected her as a little girl. Her second reaction calls upon her more mature resources, conscious of her training and competence. The dialogue often has gone like this:

Physician: "Can't you get *anything* right?"
Barbara: "Can I help you with something in particular, doctor?"
Physician: "My God, I can never find a file when I need it."
Barbara: "Which file do you need, doctor?"
Physician: "It isn't a matter of what file I need right now. It's a matter of being able to find any file at any time."
Barbara: "Doctor, the files are in order" (presuming that

they are) "and I'll be happy to assist you when you need help. Please call on me."

Barbara has kept her calm and handled a difficult person. She could have been caught in the physician's game with such responses as "Oh, I'm sorry, doctor. Things have been so hectic around here that I can't keep up" (an infantile response to "daddy" that she is incapable). In such a response, she would have followed on the physician's track of the dominating superior berating the inadequate inferior. Instead, Barbara changed the approach and attitude of the discussion so that she could deal with the physician as an equal. Neither she nor the physician might feel "good," but she, at least, does not walk away feeling "beaten" and/or "depressed." In all probability, the physician respects her, at least enough to be less critical in future encounters. This is particularly true if Barbara handles several encounters in this mature way, refusing to be treated in infantile fashion.

Another example might help. The change of approach/attitude is useful for more than handling dominating remarks. Let us suppose that the situation and attitudes above are changed. Let us suppose that Barbara is a "clinging vine," looking for somewhere or someone on which she can "cling." The discussion might take place as follows, with the physician changing the approach/attitude.

Physician: "Barbara, where are the files on Walter Smith?"

Barbara: "Aren't they under 'S,' doctor? I'm sure that's where I filed them."

Physician: "No, they aren't. Could you find them for me, please?"

Barbara: "I'll try, but you know our files better than I do. I never could figure out how Belinda (previous nurse-file clerk) set them up. I'm sorry, but I need your help."

Physician: "Barbara, it is important to our patients, as well as to me, that you know the file system."

Barbara: "Please help me, doctor."

Physician: "Call Belinda or study the files yourself. It's necessary that you are able to find what we need. I cannot help. You can do this yourself."

In this example, Barbara could have been caught up in the situation she wanted to create. The physician could have been the victim. She wanted another to do her job, so she behaved with helplessness. Had the physican responded with a sympathetic, nurturing attitude, he would have been caught. Instead, he told Barbara to do her own job, suggesting at least one way she could get help without depending on him. In this example, Barbara could become a difficult person if the physician acceded to her expressed need. He handled the situation by refusing to help where he should not be expected to help. It was a change of approach/attitude that diverted a potentially disruptive situation.

In both of these instances, feelings prompted behavior. In the first instance, the physician felt the need to dominate. In the second, the nurse felt the need to be helpless. The point is that neither feeling was appropriate. To deal with the feelings of difficult people, it is most helpful to be able to distinguish between appropriate and inappropriate feelings. There are instances when dominating feelings need to be expressed, such as expressed by the physician in the second example. There are times when dependent feelings need to be expressed, such as in those instances when we have no recourse except to find appropriate, competent help. Barbara sought assistance where it should not have been expected in the second example. The physician was dominant where it was not appropriate in the first example. The key to whether we need to change our attitude/approach or to help others to change theirs lies in areas of appropriateness. Where can we meet as adults on an equal basis or as professionals?

We need to respond in a way that is not anticipated or expected. This is another facet of changing our approach/attitude. Difficult people usually anticipate the response to their actions and/or statements. If they say "When was the last time you really contributed at a staff meeting?" they expect no response. If they say "Can't you get anything right?" they expect us to respond with a plaintive "Why? What's wrong?" If they say "I need help," they expect us to respond "How can I help you?"

Such responses can be healthy, accurate and honest, unless we know we are dealing with difficult people. This is especially true if we are dealing with people whose feelings seem unexplained, and, therefore, present a difficulty to us. We need, then, to decide whether we are dealing with people whose feelings have distorted their statements or whether we are dealing with direct people with direct questions. In the latter cases, we can respond without fear in a direct way. In the former cases, where we know we have a difficult person with whom to deal, we need to think twice about our response. We may need to respond in a way that is not anticipated.

Ed is a divisional chairman of a service organization. He holds regular staff meetings with his people. His approach is usually directive and task oriented, with occasional supportive and complimentary behavior. He does single out those who have performed well and he compliments them. For the most part, however, he is more concerned about the job to be done than about the people who do it. He frequently approaches those who have not participated actively in a staff meeting or two, following the meeting, and he makes such remarks as "You've been quiet recently. Is there a problem?" or "When was the last time you really contributed to a staff meeting?" Usually, the response is "No problem!" or "I haven't had anything to say." This usually brings on a tirade about interest in the job, loyalty to the company, and "pulling your weight."

Recently, he approached Bernie, who chose not to allow himself to be subjected to such a tirade. Bernie responded in a way Ed did not expect.

Ed: "Bernie, you've been pretty quiet at the last few staff meetings. Is there a problem?"

Bernie: "Frankly, yes, Ed, I have a problem, but I'm not sure I can discuss it with you without becoming more of a problem. I need to talk with you as a friend or as an equal, not as a subordinate to a superior. Can we do that?

Ed: "I'm not sure. We can't change facts, can we? But I would like to know what's bothering you."

Bernie: "O.K. I feel that any contribution I make at the staff meeting is already judged by your own previous decisions. You don't seem to want contributions unless they support what you've already decided."

Ed: "I never looked at it that way. I always thought I was open."

The discussion certainly continued and, depending upon the responses of both Ed and Bernie, became helpful or not. The salient fact is that Bernie did not respond as expected and took the risk of dealing with a person he found difficult. When we take such a risk, there is no guarantee of success, so that we need to be aware of the consequences and to be willing to handle them. A favorable outcome usually depends on our own ability to remain within the realm of reason and logic without allowing our feelings to dictate our behavior. At the same time, we need to appreciate that our unanticipated responses arouse the feelings of the other and we need to be prepared to deal with those feelings in a constructive way.

Whether we are willing to take this kind of risk or not depends on the importance the issue has in our own perspective.

There are times when we can use the unexpected response with little risk to ourselves or to others, such as when our response is playful. Usually, if the situation or issue is not serious, a playful response is very effective. It seems to be most effective in situations where the relationship between the people involved is healthy and trusting most of the time.

Cort, a male secretary, often works closely with Carol, the clerk typist in the same department. Usually they get along well. There are times, however, when one or the other becomes a difficult person. Cort, on occasion, expects too much of Carol: "Carol, aren't those letters typed YET? They should have been done an hour ago!" Carol sometimes responds: "Yes,

Master! You are the all-patient one. Have mercy!" and successfully averts a ruckus. When, on occasion, Carol becomes difficult, Cort has been known to say, "Hey, practicing your
nastiness? Guess you expect to join the bosses soon. In your
mood, you'd fit right in!"

When we change our approach/attitude and respond in a
way not expected, we also *change the subject so that the difficult area of discussion is put aside.* If we study the examples
above, we can find this criterion fulfilled. In the first example
of Barbara and the irate physician the area of difficulty is the
accused incompetency of Barbara to handle the files; she
forces the subject to be the order of the files by her responses.
In the second example, nurse Barbara poses the area of difficulty as her own need to depend on inappropriate others; the
physician changes the subject to how she can handle such unnecessary dependence.

In the example of Ed and Bernie, the area of difficulty is
Ed's habit of berating others unnecessarily. Bernie turns the
subject around to Ed's style of meeting behavior and its consequences. In the examples of Cort and Carol the areas of difficulty are over-domination by Cort and nasty remarks by Carol.
Both can change the subject around to their basically good relationship by using a playful response.

By their very nature the change of approach/attitude or
the unexpected response changes the subject to an area that
we can control more easily and discuss more reasonably than
the difficulty that is filled with emotions, often feelings of supe-
riority and inferiority. The subject we change to may still need
delicate treatment and control of feelings, such as in the Ed
and Bernie situation, but it generally lends itself more easily to
logic and constructive discussion.

Our manner of behavior, tone of voice and verbal emphasis all play a part in making the response that will turn the subject to a less difficult level. We need to be aware of our own
feelings and to sense the feelings of the other with some accu-
racy. In our first example, for instance, Barbara could have responded to the angry physician: "(sigh) Can I help you with

something *IN PARTICULAR, doctor?"* looking at him with fire in her eyes. The words are the same as those that allowed Barbara to raise the discussion to a cognitive level, but the intonation would probably negate the reasonable response and turn the situation into an uproar, the physician demanding more respect, etc.

We need to respond verbally and non-verbally in a way that helps us to feel good about ourselves and, at least, allows the other person to attain the same feeling. We do not want to play the game of "Now I've Got You, You Son of a Bitch," as described in Transactional Analysis. We simply exercise our right to straight transactions without "Game playing," the right to protect ourselves and the right to express ourselves so that we retain control of our own feelings and behavior. In effect, we have the right to use those facets of our personality that enable us to maintain healthy, level relationships with others, as far as it is humanly possible.

SURVIVAL STRATEGIES

1. Get your Adult in gear when difficult feelings surface. Make a choice to ignore them (i.e., not to make an issue of them) or to deal with them.
2. Often we can deal with difficult feelings by
   a. changing the situation by
   b. responding in unexpected ways so that
   c. the difficult subject and accompanying feelings are sidetracked.

Summary

Feelings play a large part in our coping with difficult people, since not only do we have the other's feelings to consider, but we need also be aware of our own. To recognize and to accept our own feelings is fundamental in a difficult relationship.

All of us feel; if we think that we do not, we have to look a little deeper, grow a little more sensitive and, perhaps, be more honest with ourselves.

At the same time, we do not have to let others determine our feelings. We choose to be angry or not over a false accusation or to be fearful or not in the face of threat. We can often find possible reasons for the behavior of others that can soften or change our feelings.

Recent studies suggest that, contrary to popular opinion, it is not always helpful to express our feelings, to strive for a catharsis or to "talk them out." Sometimes such efforts only intensify feelings. It may be best to distract ourselves with other interests. Hostile feelings, at least, seem to dissipate more quickly this way.

Difficult feelings can also be somewhat lessened by understanding some of the syndromes of difficult people. They may be feeling depressed, guilty, fearful, etc., and refuse to admit such feelings even to themselves. They may have been raised in an environment that discouraged a healthy handling of difficult feelings. Perhaps the reasons for difficult people are as varied as people themselves. It helps us, however, to look at a few possible explanations for difficult behavior, as we did in this chapter. People may be crying for help by redefining everything we say or by using a racket that lends them some of the support they need. We may not be able to help such difficult people change, but understanding can make them less difficult to us.

We do have the right to protect ourselves, however, when we meet difficult people one-on-one. We have ways to redirect the discussion, so that we can communicate more reasonably: we can change our approach/attitude, since we know that while we may accept our anger, fear, etc., we do not have to act on it. Often we change our approach by responding in an unexpected, reasonable, Adult fashion, with the result that we change the subject away from areas of difficulties to areas of reason, logic and constructive exchange of observations and ideas.

It is now time to reflect on difficult people in groups, to learn some things we can do to make such people less destructive to group activity and productivity. We need to keep in mind much of what has been said, since people in groups carry with them all of their unique personality and individuality. But, as we shall see, coping with difficult people in groups or dealing with difficult groups has a dimension all its own.

7

Difficult People in Groups

It is one thing to deal with a difficult person in a normal work or family situation. It is another thing to deal with a difficult person in a group. A group may be described as "a set of persons (by definition or observation) among whom there exists a definable or observable set of relations . . . a set of mutually interdependent behavioral systems that not only affect each other, but respond to exterior influences as well. The notion of a group may seem less mysterious if it is imagined to be composed, first, of a set of persons, and second, of a collection of interdependent persons" (J.H. Davis, *Group Performance*, Addison-Wesley Publishing Co., Reading, Mass., 1969, p. 4). This description might refer to a family, as well as to a business group, church group or interest group. While I have dealt with the family groups in some detail in Chapter 4, I do not exclude them in this chapter. Human behavior is really too complex to place in compartments.

For purposes of this chapter, groups include any collection of individuals oriented to a common purpose or mutually dependent in one way or another by a common bond: work, relationship, interest, conviction, purpose, etc.

During the past two and a half decades, most group studies have focused on groups in business, perhaps because they have been the most available groups for study. Many conclusions have been based on the observation and analysis of group meetings in the business situation. Some such conclusions have indicated that fewer difficulties arise where group members are slow to criticize, reluctant to place blame, employees are not made to feel inferior, and leaders tend to be flexible and to be primarily concerned about their people, rather than themselves. Business groups that indicated these characteristics generally functioned more productively than those that exhibited opposite tendencies (cf. R. Likert, *New Patterns of Management*, McGraw-Hill Book Co., N.Y., 1961, pp. 138–139).

Allowing for the obvious differences between a business group and volunteer, religious, education, political and interest groups, we can still see some lessons to be learned from this kind of research.

(1) Persons react more constructively when they do not fear ready criticism, especially of a negative kind.

(2) Persons are more willing to take risks in groups where there is less readiness to place blame.

(3) Persons do not like to feel inferior; when they do, they are more disposed to be negative and dysfunctional.

(4) Persons do not respond well to stubborn leaders.

(5) Persons need to feel that they are appreciated and valued.

An additional and valuable insight into difficulties in groups has been contributed by F.E. Fiedler in his research report *A Theory of Leadership Effectiveness* (McGraw-Hill Book Co., N.Y., 1967). He suggests that accurate perception of others within a group is not desirable if we are seeking the best means to healthy and productive interpersonal relationships within the group: " ... accurate, objective but unfavorable perceptions may be less desirable for many good relationships than inaccurate but favorable perceptions. Most people want to be accepted for what they would like to be, not for what they really are" (p. 39). In this context he asks whether a child, viewed by his or her parents accurately as stubborn and disobedient, will relate better within the family than the child who is perceived inaccurately as charming, well-behaved and intelligent. Fielder suggests that better relationships will more likely be found where the perceptions are favorable, although inaccurate. From both experience and theory, I tend to agree with him.

Preventing Difficulties

Not long ago I belonged to a regional group that seemed to have more than its share of difficulties. Our mandate was to create a program that would expose educators to new curricula, teaching methods and recent educational philosophy, so we were not political in any strict sense of the word. Since politics is often built upon competition, rather than cooperation, I probably would not have been surprised by some of the difficulties that surfaced, had we been a political group. But we were not political.

Still, I found a good deal of distrust, guarded communication, unspoken competition and an inability to handle conflict in any constructive way. Larry, a psychologist, seemed too frequently attacked by Ray, a high school principal: "That's O.K., I guess, as a theory, but it isn't true in the real world" was a characteristic response of Ray to much of what Larry contributed. Although there were eight people in the group, four or five generally dominated any discussion. The leader seemed more interested in maintaining friendliness and a surface of tranquillity than in clarifying goals and objectives. He gave the impression of weakness. Needless to say, the group accomplished little and its report was not acted upon.

Looking back on the experience, I think I would have tried harder to help the people confront some of the incipient problems if I had suspected their presence and the destructive effect they would have on the group. Somehow I would convince the group to spend a little time reflecting on the process of the group. Probably I would do this by talking to some individuals, trying to solicit their backing. I would then make some suggestions in the group, such as having all complete the "Group Norms Continuum" on page 156 about the second or third meeting. We would share our perceptions and talk over ways to handle difficulties or misunderstandings that seemed to surface. I would suggest that we all spend the last ten or fifteen minutes of each meeting reflecting on what happened in that particular meeting, whether we were satisfied with the session and what we want to repeat or change in future sessions.

This can be an effective way of preventing difficulties in groups. If we can prevent them, we need not deal with them.

Using such a continuum we can head off many potential difficulties. The continuum may be completed anonymously, especially if we feel that we shall get truer responses this way. When completed, the forms are collected and collated on large sheets of paper or on a blackboard. This may be done by a person outside of and even unknown to the group; the person may not even know what group he or she is dealing with. The findings are then shared by all. We will need to discuss those items where there are wide differences in the ratings. Such diversity usually indicates very different perceptions and/or expectations that need to be clarified and unified. We need also to look carefully at items that most members rate poorly, since it is very likely that there is some truth to such consistent low ratings and we need to agree on ways to improve to the satisfaction of the group members.

The collated continuum can be posted at each meeting and can be the basis for the reflection period at the end of each meeting. After six weeks or so, all may take the continuum again. Findings are newly collated and compared with earlier perceptions to indicate progress or continuing difficulties. The reflection periods then use these new findings as a basis for their discussions.

I have found this process, since my experience described above, to be far easier to deal with than the difficulties that arise where it (or a process like it) is absent. It seems threatening for only a short period of time.

Group Norms Continuum

Now that we have worked together a little, most of us are likely to have formed some conclusions about our group. Your perceptions are valuable. Please rate the group on the items below on a scale of 1 to 10 (1 being low and 10 being high). For the benefit of all and for the productivity of our work, be as honest as you can. No name is expected on this sheet. Circle the number you see describing us. *As you see it,* is there in our group:

1. very little trust   1 2 3 4 5 6 7 8 9 10   much trust

2. no concern for
   each other   1 2 3 4 5 6 7 8 9 10   much concern for
   each other

3. reluctance to
   communicate
   openly   1 2 3 4 5 6 7 8 9 10   open
   communication

4. lack of clarity of
   goals   1 2 3 4 5 6 7 8 9 10   clarity of goals

5. no commitment
   to our goals   1 2 3 4 5 6 7 8 9 10   full commitment to
   our goals

6. failure to use well
   the abilities of
   our members   1 2 3 4 5 6 7 8 9 10   good use of the
   abilities of our
   members

7. failure to handle
   conflict well   1 2 3 4 5 6 7 8 9 10   good handling of
   conflict

8. domination of our
   discussions by a
   few   1 2 3 4 5 6 7 8 9 10   no domination of
   our discussions by a
   few

9. a lot of pressure
   to conform   1 2 3 4 5 6 7 8 9 10   a lot of respect for
   individual
   differences

Difficulties can also be prevented at times if members, or at least the leader of the group, will be aware of how groups seem to develop, the stages that can be expected as a group matures.

Cog's Ladder is one theory of group development worth knowing. The first phase of development, according to Cog, is the *Polite* stage. People tend to avoid controversy, share acceptable ideas and avoid serious discussion. We can avoid possible difficulty by accepting this phase as legitimate. It is not a waste of time. People need to begin to feel comfortable with each other and to "get to know" one another before they are ready for business. Trying to skip this phase or allowing no time for it will generally cause difficulties later. It is a good time to agree on some "ground rules" among the members, such as "honesty that is responsible is acceptable," "individual differences are acceptable," etc.

The second stage of development is the *Purpose* stage, usually signaled by one or more group members asking: "Well, what are we here for? What are we supposed to do?" Sometimes the purpose of the group is given to it by "outside" authority. At other times, the group has to clarify its own purpose. In either case, future difficulties can be avoided by using some time to elicit the feelings of group members about the purpose. Wider commitment to the purpose of the group can be encouraged in this way, especially by making the purpose clearly understood by all in the same way.

The third stage of group growth is the *Power* stage. It is a phase in which members usually make a bid to have some influence over the procedures and life of the group. The bid might be as insignificant as urging the group to schedule meetings a half hour shorter, or it might be as significant as questioning the competence of the leader. Legitimate competition is taking place and needs to be handled if the group is not to become stalled at this point and sow seeds of serious difficulty. It is important, first and foremost, to recognize that this is a legitimate phase of group development. It is not a vicious attack on the group or on the leader. People feel the need and have the right to control their activity constructively. They have the right to have some influence over work that costs them time and effort. If this phase is passed over without resolution, if attempts are made to bury the "bids" with laughter or ridicule, people remain uncommitted to the group and even become hostile and dysfunctional. The "bids" need to be taken seriously, responded to and resolved with as much satisfaction as possible. Otherwise, the group never really passes this stage. Some work may be done by such a group, but is generally of poor quality and members don't enjoy being with the group. There usually is a high "turnover" in such a group.

On occasion, a group member may overdo this need for control. We shall discuss this difficulty in the next section. Usually, more is involved than a stage of group development.

A fourth phase of development, according to Cog, is the *Constructive* stage, in which members work well together, listen to each other, clarify issues, and exhibit mutual trust, mutual support and respect. Few difficulties arise when a group achieves this maturity. The one difficulty of which members need to be aware is the difficulty of maintaining this level of development. It is possible to slip back into "power struggles" or even a conflict of purposes.

A fifth phase of development is the *Esprit* stage. Morale is high among group members. They have strong loyalty to and take great pride in their group. They can often accomplish more than is expected or can be explained by the individual talents of group members. My experience with hundreds of groups has indicated that many like to think they have achieved this stage. In fact, I think only a few are so successful. There are few difficulties during this phase. The addition of even one new member, however, can destroy the Esprit stage and require the group to begin building anew from an earlier phase.

Another element useful for preventing difficulties from arising within groups is leadership style: fitting the style of leadership to the maturity (or immaturity) of the group. Paul Hersey and Kenneth H. Blanchard have written extensively about this under the title of situational leadership (*Management of Organizational Behavior,* 2nd edition, Prentice-Hall, Inc., Englewood Cliffs, N.J., 1972). Since I have dealt with this concept in a previous publication, I shall be brief, considering it only in the light of preventing group difficulties (cf. C.J. Keating, *The Leadership Book,* revised edition, Paulist Press, N.Y., N.Y., 1982).

A mature group is one that is psychologically, not necessarily chronologically, mature. Members know their task, organize, plan and implement it with good listening, mutual support and open communication. They may not be in the Esprit stage, but they are, at least, in the Constructive stage of development. They need leadership that respects their expertise, facilitates them when useful, but does not try to be strongly directive. Such a group bristles under directive leadership and difficulties arise.

An immature group has lost its purpose, is poor in planning, organizing and implementing its task, has low morale and little sense of direction. Without strong, directive leadership difficulties will probably continue to multiply until the group disintegrates. Attempting to lead this group the way one would successfully lead a mature group will intensify the problems it has.

Perhaps most groups are of average maturity. Members may do some things well and other things poorly. They may be highly task oriented. Leadership then needs to supply a good deal of encouragement and support, thereby deepening the cohesiveness of the members to each other. Or a group may be strong in mutual support and encouragement, such as may be found in some social groups like country clubs or sororities/fraternities. If this group faces a task, it needs a leader who will supply strong task orientation, clarifying purposes, offering structures to accomplish the task and controlling the progress of the task. If such a group should be unfortunate enough to get a leader who offers only more interpersonal support, frustration, depression and failure will probably be its lot.

The point is that leadership always needs to supply the needs of the group, doing what the group is not doing for itself. The leader who misreads a group, who duplicates what the group is already doing well or who does not have the skills to provide what is lacking will be responsible for creating many difficulties in the life of that group. Good prevention of difficulties often amounts to good judgment and skills of the leader.

There are groups that need the leader to supply EVERYTHING, both task orientation and group cohesiveness, at least initially. The leader needs to perform, sincerely, in such a manner that members will copy his or her behavior. As the behavior is "picked up" by group members a good deal of support and encouragement is required from the leader if future difficulties are to be avoided. Surprisingly, these groups are usually of average maturity, but lacking sufficient task and relationship functions. They do a little of each, but not enough of either. They, for instance, may be clear and committed to goals, but not know the structures to accomplish them. They may be friendly and encouraging, but not know how to build on each other's ideas. The leader needs to have an educated judgment and the skill to fill the needs perceived.

Handling Group Difficulties

If you are an "intuitive" in the sense of Myers-Briggs, as described in Chapter 1, you will have enjoyed the above discussion. If you are a "sensing" personality, you will enjoy the following. We can do much to prevent difficulties from arising in groups, be we "sensing" or "intuitive." The rest of this chapter, regardless of whether we are "intuitive" or "sensing," should be of help. We shall deal with the "nuts and bolts" of group operation. We shall deal with difficulties that can arise no matter how well we work for common expectations and perceptions, how cognizant we are of group development or how capable our leadership may be. Group difficulties are pervasive and constant because human behavior cannot be programmed. People will be people.

I do not pretend to deal with *all* the difficulties that can develop in groups. We shall discuss those that I have found most frequent: (1) the person who talks too much, (2) the person is *too* quick and "helpful," (3) those who almost always ask the opinion of the leader before discussion can really develop, (4) the bored individual, (5) the person who "just wants to listen" and didn't come to talk, (6) the shy, hesitant member, (7) the individual not disposed to help others, (8) the side conversationalist, (9) the person with a poor voice or a poor choice of words, (10) the individual who is definitely wrong but certain of his or her facts, (11) those with personality conflicts, (12) the rambler, (13) the arguer, (14) the person who is frequently off-the-subject, (15) those who persist with gripes about management/authority even though the group cannot effectively deal with these issues, and (16) the individual with a problem of his or her own not relevant to the group.

Also, I am sure there are ways other than I suggest to handle even this sample of group difficulties. I share what I have found to be effective in helping a group to be productive and satisfied.

Situation: Debbie *talks too much* at group sessions. During any given hour, Debbie will talk half of the time. Her contributions are useful and frequent, but they do prevent others from thinking and expressing their thoughts. She does not dominate with speeches or diatribes, but she does speak whenever there is a lull in the discussion. She seems to abhor a silence. As a result, important ideas are sometimes lost, since she does not build on what was previously said, or her patter interrupts the train of thought of others in the group.

Strategy: Be attentive to Debbie, since she probably has some good ideas. She is interested and willing to risk suggestions. When she pauses, cut in with a statement like "Those things are certainly worth considering (providing you think that they are; don't be phony). Thank you. Perhaps others want to build on what you've said, or to add some thoughts of their own. Anyone else?" Also, look to areas away from Debbie for contributions from the group. Don't ignore her all the time. If you do you will lose her, and you don't want to lose the contributions of any group member. You do, however, have to control the contributions that inhibit other contributions. Carefully timed, your intervention may be made as group leader or group member.

Situation: Jimmy *wants to be helpful and quickly responds* to any request for ideas. He is the first to contribute, usually. But you sense, as leader or member, that he is regularly shaping the group and leading it in a particular direction, perhaps without intending to do so. He just wants to be an active member. Or he may intend to direct the group in this subtle way.

Strategy: You don't want to lose Jimmy any more than you want to lose Debbie, so voice appreciation for his suggestions. You do want to give others a chance to lead off the discussion, since you feel that there are probably other facets that need consideration. As a new topic is brought up, look away from Jimmy to encourage others to make the first contribution. You may even use light humor (provided there is sufficient trust in the group) such as "We've been working you too hard. How about a response from others to start us thinking?" This strategy is best used by the leader. Members can help by more prompt responses.

Situation: Jean has a *habit of asking the opinion of the leader or of the "authority figure" in the group before discussion can really get underway.* The result, often, is that group members feel no need to contribute and the group process is stymied. The end result is that the leader or "authority figure" could have saved a lot of people a lot of time by sitting alone and making decisions. The other members feel reluctant to disagree or add to the opinions voiced by the "authority." Some members feel relieved. Others feel frustrated, seeing their time and effort being wasted. Usually attendance drops and the group ceases to exist.

Strategy: The leader or "authority figure" can handle this situation most easily by redirecting the question Jean asks to the group: "What does the group think about this?" But, again, don't be phony. If there is no answer to Jean's question, say so. Don't lead the group on a wild goose chase. Members can also help by waiting for the "authority figure" to share his or her opinion and then saying something like: "That is valuable information (if it is), and I think we can build on it. It seems to me ..." or "I think ... and I wonder how other members react." The strategy is to be supportive while not allowing any one group member, authority or not, to dominate a group's direction and decision.

Situation: The member seems to be *bored or indifferent.* You know that all group members need to be heard; otherwise there was no need to include them in the first place. You see a valuable asset being lost. You feel that if the situation is not remedied, this member will drop out of the group. If you feel that would be best for the group do nothing.

Strategy: If you want this member to remain with the group, call on him or her, pointing out his or her competence, experience or expertise on one or the other topics of discussion: "Eleanor, you've had some experience with. . . . Do you want to add anything to what has been said?" Don't put Eleanor on the spot with a remark like: "Eleanor, we haven't heard from you all evening. Don't you have anything to say?" Rather, try to focus on a strength of Eleanor and ask for her contribution from that base. Sometimes people simply need to be told that they are valued and appreciated.

Situation: Paul has been *quiet and non-contributing for quite a while.* He seems successful, competent and positive to you, so there is some concern about his behavior. You don't want to lose him, since you see him as a valuable asset to the group. Yet his silence seems to you to be a premonition of his leaving the group.

Strategy: Some people find it difficult to speak in a group. Not everyone contributes at the same frequency. Don't push Paul too hard. Encourage him occasionally, so that he knows that you feel his contribution is valuable. Say something like: "Does anyone else have anything to add. (*Look at Paul.*) There is a great deal of expertise in this group, and we would like to utilize all of it." Some people come to a group to listen long and hard before they become involved. It is less important that they talk readily than that they stay close to the group. Be patient. If such people are made to feel they are valuable, that their contributions are welcome, they will respond.

Situation: The *shy, hesitant individual* is not always easy to distinguish from the "Pauls" described immediately before. The difference is that the shy individual doesn't choose not to contribute. He or she is afraid to contribute. Sylvia, for instance, was a housewife. She was shy in a group where I was teaching Transactional Analysis. The other members were mostly teachers and professional people. Sylvia was not used to speaking in groups, much less to speaking among "professional" people. Yet Sylvia had a great deal to contribute, especially when we spoke about human relationships.

Strategy: Ask direct questions that you think the "Sylvias" can answer. Support their responses, if you can honestly, and elaborate on their contributions when possible. Build up Sylvia in the eyes of the group and in her own eyes: "That's good (*if it is*). I had never thought of it that way (*if you haven't*)."

Situation: Some individuals, by reason of experience or aptitude, are *not disposed to help others*. They feel that they have given too much and received too little in their lives, perhaps, so they choose to "lie back." They want others to "pull their own weight" and not to depend on them. They may be jaded, hurt, disappointed or simply tired.

Strategy: This kind of person needs to be recognized, so it may take a few sessions to determine where he or she is. Once you have decided that this may be the problem, however, it is time to act, since such a person is probably a very valuable asset. Before the next session, let him or her know how much you appreciate having him or her in the group and how much you think he or she can contribute to the group in the light of his or her experience and background. During the session, draw him or her out with such statements as: "Linda, do you have anything to add in the light of your own experience with . . ." Thank Linda for any contribution she might make. But don't be disturbed if your first efforts receive a "no" from Linda. Give her time. Continue to speak to her about group issues before or after sessions.

Situation: One or more group members might have the *habit of holding conversations on the side* with other group members during the working session. They are the "whisperers." Usually, they are a source of considerable distraction, particularly if they do this often.

Strategy: If you are the group member with whom they choose to whisper, the strategy is rather easy. Simply let them know that you want to give full attention to what is happening in the group. If you are the one being distracted, let them know that you can't concentrate on what is going on because of their talking. As the leader of the group you can pause and look in their direction the first or second time you see side conversations happening. If the conversations continue, you can be more direct: "Vince, I didn't hear what you said. Do you want to share something with the group?" Do this sincerely, since sharing might be exactly what Vince wants. You can also walk down to the location of the whisperer and draw the attention of the group to him or her in this way, provided that your session allows you to walk about as a matter of course. The goal is to let the whisperer know that this kind of behavior is not acceptable in this group, without making a big issue of it, since that would only be more distracting.

Situation: Occasionally you will have a group member with either a *poor voice or a poor choice of words*. In both instances, there is a possibility of losing valuable insights or of misunderstandings. Such a person might mumble, or he or she might not feel as educated as others in the group and find it difficult to find the right words to voice his or her thoughts.

Strategy: If necessary, protect such members from ridicule in the group. When it is honestly possible, give their ideas recognition and support. Repeat what you understand them to be saying in your own words: "In other words, you are saying ..." or "Let me see if I understand you correctly. You are saying ..." Any group member can help in this way. If no help is forthcoming, it is likely that these kind of members will soon be lost to the group. In some instances, it might be helpful to simply ask the member to speak a little louder.

Situation: A group member may be *definitely wrong* about facts or events but unwilling to be corrected. Such members are certain they are right and no one can tell them differently. If a correction is attempted, a debate is likely to ensue and time may be unnecessarily consumed. If no correction is attempted, wrong information might mislead the group and damage their work.

Strategy: If the wrong information is irrelevant to the group and to its work, simply acknowledge that such members have spoken, with something like: "O.K. Thank you," and go on with the agenda. If their error concerns areas already covered by the group, such as group consensus or group research, recall what the group has decided or concluded and close with: "Well, the group has already made some decisions about that point, but yours may be another way of looking at it." Then go on. If their error, however, could damage group work or occasion a loss of group members, it will be important to take the time to clarify the error or misunderstanding with verified facts, reference to authorities or a review of past minutes. It is possible that more members than the speaker have misunderstood.

Some members of a group in which I participated recently, for instance, kept referring to the "office Christmas party" which the group had decided not to hold this year. It became obvious that some members anticipated and were preparing for the party. As it turned out, these people had not been present when the decision to drop the party had been made, and it was necessary to go through the decision making process again, when they were present. The alternative would have been to have these people frustrated and disappointed, perhaps feeling "railroaded." This would not have been good for the group. Time for debate or redecisioning can be helpful and sometimes necessary for group health.

Situation: *Personality clashes* are a real possibility, as we have seen in Chapter 1. Brenda is a "thinker," while Virginia is a "feeler." They frequently see things quite differently, Brenda looking at the logic and reason of the issue and Virginia looking at how she and others feel about the issue. Both are good workers, believing in efficiency and taking pride in their work. Brenda has the habit of correcting a fellow worker on the spot of the perceived error. This irritates Virginia, who feels that there is a time and place for correction. That place, for instance, is not in the presence of others. Conflict arises when Virginia criticizes Brenda for the way she has treated a friend of Virginia's. But this is only one example of their personality conflict. They even carry the clash into their Quality Circle. They get "carried away" in anger and the work of the Circle suffers.

Strategy: Another group member or the leader needs to cut into the dispute by pointing out that there are certainly different ways of looking at a topic, and both Brenda's and Virginia's perceptions can be valuable to the group: "We need to see differences as enrichments, not as problems." If the dispute has concentrated on personal attacks, there may be a need to ask directly that personalities be "left out of the discussion for the time being, at least, and that we focus on the topic itself." If personality problems arise in an on-going, long-term group, it could be useful for all to complete the Myers-Briggs personality indicator I have discussed in Chapter 1. One of the conclusions of Myers-Briggs research is that groups made up of different personality types are more likely to be successful than groups composed of members of similar personalities. In this sense, if properly understood and appreciated, personality "conflict" can become an asset, rather than a problem, for a group.

Situation: The *rambler* is the group member who begins to speak on the topic but soon turns to other interests, ruminating about old experiences, reflecting on recently read articles or mentioning irrelevant experiences. He or she needs an audience and uses the group situation to procure one. Ramblers find it difficult to stick to a topic, giving in to the temptation to flow with their own train of thought. They are not unlike a "flow of consciousness" that used to be an accepted literary style. Lillian, a woman of eighty-three years of age, was a member of one of my recent groups. She was mentally alert and filled with a wealth of wisdom. One night a topic of great interest to her arose: the stock market. "We have been in stock a good number of years—maybe fifty, I guess," she said, "and I support it. Our group might be small, but if we put our resources together, we can be BIG. I remember when my husband and I started out with only two stocks; that was in 1950—we were along in years even at that time. Well, let me tell you, we were scared. Both of us had been through the depression and . . ." And so it goes. The rambler can consume great gobs of time with little effect.

Strategy: The rambler might have a great deal to offer, but it needs to be focused and ordered. Lillian was full of wisdom, but the group had to learn how to tap the wisdom without too much consumption of time. Certainly there is a value in giving an audience to the rambler, be they eighteen or eighty, since all of us need an audience at one time or another. Any group has to allow for individuals who need the group as a sounding board. But there are limits. One way to handle the rambler in a group is to intervene as he or she stops for breath. Thank him or her for their suggestions, rephrase the last of the statements made and QUICKLY move to others in the group (unless you want more from the rambler, which could be possible if you sense wisdom on its way). Quickly call the attention of the group to the topic, soliciting contributions from others, even if they have not volunteered. If useful, give your own reflections on the topic until other group members have put their thoughts together. Don't "put down" the rambler. Some of the best ramblers I have known have been brilliant and insightful people. On the other hand, don't feel that your group needs to "put up" with the rambler. If he or she has wisdom, it will surface. Ramblers are persistent.

Situation: The *arguer,* like Donna, enjoys dispute. He or she finds life dull without an argument. Donna joins groups so that she can find people with whom she disagrees. "I totally disagree" is one of Donna's favorite statements. One evening I counted her disagreements to be twenty. Since everyone expected this behavior from Donna, no one reacted. Only occasionally, and in highly emotional situations, did anyone "take Donna on." At the moment it is not our concern to determine why Donna was so negative. Previous chapters, such as Chapters 2 and 3, might suggest some reasons. The question here is how to deal with Donnas and still be productive as a group.

Strategy: Don't take Donnas for granted, ignoring their behavior as typical. This solves nothing. It only perpetuates Donna's behavior. Recognize Donna's legitimate objections, ask for clarifications and support her insights when honestly possible. "That's a valid objection and we need to handle it" is a good response if we want to take Donna seriously and help her with her negative attitude. When the group needs to be evaluative, rather than creative, Donnas are needed. They may foresee problems ignored by others in their enthusiasm. The more attention paid to Donnas, the less negative they become, but they never relinquish their evaluative stance. As long as Donnas have no ax "to grind" they can be helpful.

If they do have an ax "to grind," place them in the "blind spot," beside you. Pretend not to hear. Their loss will ordinarily not be consequential, unless they have powerful associations.

If Donnas have an ax "to grind," have considerable connections and persist in their argumentative attitude, talk to them before the next session, asking for their help or giving them a specific task for the session: "Donna, I need someone to take notes on the newsprint during tonight's discussion. Would you do that for me?" If Donna rebels at this primitive effort, level with her, sharing how you feel her behavior is affecting the group and asking for her support. "If you can't support us, that's fine, because we need your analytical talent. But I ask that you be positive where you can."

When these efforts are not effective, call on the group for help: "As I understand Donna, she is concerned about . . . Does the group feel that it wants to spend time now on these objections?" Keep calm and rational. As member or leader, don't let Donna turn the session into a donnybrook. There may come a moment when Donna clearly does not belong in this group. Her departure, however, should be her choice. The alternative is a stigma on the group as Donna spreads her version of the confrontation. In any case, it seems to me, the group should not retaliate, but it might prepare itself to answer to higher authority where appropriate.

Situation: Most groups have a member, who frequently *speaks off-the-subject.* Such members are a lot like the rambler described above, but they differ from the rambler in that they do not even begin talking on the subject. Statements often begin with "That reminds me of . . ." or "This is like when . . ." Ken, a member in one group I know of, makes a number of contributions to his group, but fifty percent of them have to do with TV production, even when TV does not fit into the topic under disussion. Ken is a TV camera operator.

Strategy: Generally this is an easy situation to handle, since such members, like Ken, are not hostile or indifferent. Often they only have an overwhelming interest in their jobs, hobbies or past experiences. Listen for a time, but at the first opportunity, such as a pause, say: "Those are interesting points. Could we take them up at another time and concentrate now on . . ." If at all possible, try to get back to some of the points the member has made, since you did suggest taking them up at another time. Refer to some point of Ken's for instance, when it is more appropriate: "Ken made a point about . . . a little while ago and it might be helpful to recall it here . . ." If the contribution of the off-the-subject member is so off-the-subject that you foresee no way of considering it, even later, make no promises: "I like what you're saying, but right now we need to get back to the agenda. We don't have a great deal of time."

Situation: *Gripes about management/authority* lead to problems when management/authority is beyond the parameters and competence of the group. Obviously, this could become a gripe session if left unhandled. It is a particular danger, it seems, in the early life of a group. Somehow people tend to blame management/authority for all ills, and sometimes they may be right. To begin by blaming, however, is to court disaster for most groups. There are few ready answers, authority is usually strongly entrenched and resistant to criticism, and the group soon finds itself buried in negative opinions and feelings. The group is not anxious to meet again. No one seeks frustration.

Strategy: The group needs to recognize what it can accomplish within limitations. It needs to recognize worthwhile goals that can be achieved within the present management/authority perimeter. Its task needs clarification and the group needs to feel committed to that task, feeling good about being able to do something useful, although it knows it cannot do everything. There are members, of course, who find such limitations most difficult to accept. Kevin, for instance, calls any group that tries to accomplish ANYTHING while there are serious problems with management/authority outside of the group a halfway group. He rarely joins such groups, but when he does his contributions are "Nothing can be done until we get a new manager (president, board of directors, etc.)" or "Why waste our time when we know Mr. Bramble is the problem? Get him out and all our problems will disappear."

Several efforts might be made to make Kevin a functional group member: (1) personal persuasion, one-on-one, that something can be done, even in the present system, (2) an appeal to "let's do something, even though we know some problems will still be with us," (3) suggesting that what the group can accomplish will affect management/authority eventually (if you think it will), or (4) helping him to see that in this business, management/authority needs to act the way they do (if you believe this to be true).

If Kevin's remarks are valid, acknowledge them to be so, but move the group along by calling on the support of other members to recognize that criticism of management/authority is not the task of this group at the present. "We want to do what we can in a positive way."

Of course, if the change or modification of management/authority is part of the group's task, criticism of them is acceptable. Even then, however, this area is so fraught with strong feelings that it is usually necessary to agree on a good structure or method of approaching the topic before discussion begins.

Situation: Jon really has an inferiority complex. He swings between cringing in the background and "spilling his guts" in front of the group to convince the other members that he is suffering unjust, degrading and hurtful treatment by them as well as by others. He is so taken up with his *personal problem* that he cannot become concerned about the work of the group. On more than one occasion he has given a tirade of more than twenty minutes. Usually he did not attend the next few meetings after these outbursts.

Strategy: A personal problem needs to be handled personally, so it is often best to speak with this kind of member privately. In addition, it is important not to allow the member to say things in the group that he or she will later be sorry that he or she shared. At times, therefore, it is necessary to ask the member to stop talking and to promise to speak with him or her later. There may be no gracious way to handle the situation.

There may be some rare occasion when group members feel that they can help the personal problem member, particularly if his or her problem has some relationship to the group. If the group members have some training or experience with counseling, perhaps discussing the individual's personal problem in the group may be helpful. Ordinarily, however, a group should not be expected to take on this kind of task, even with confidentiality assured. Certainly no new group should attempt such "treatment."

In most instances of this kind, the best thing a group member can do is to help protect the personal problem member from himself or herself by restricting too much personal sharing. The group should then move on with its work.

All of this, of course, presumes that the group has not been established as a therapeutic or sensitivity group, whose task it would be to share and to help with personal problems.

Jon, in the example cited in our "situation," might have benefited most in his tirades if some member of the group volunteered: "Jon, it sounds as though you need to share something important and serious with the group, but could I talk to you first, privately after our session? I feel I can help."

While most problems in groups require individual solutions, there are some general rules for handling group problems that are useful to keep in mind. (1) If the problem arises in group *meetings,* look for issues or conflicts within the organization, community or system that might occasion the problem. The system, for instance, might provide no procedure for expressing concerns, anxieties or gripes. These, therefore, come out in meetings not designed for them. In such a case, the system needs to initiate ways that concerns can be voiced productively. (2) Group members who are willing to help resolve group member problems need to stay in their ADULT, using reason and logic, using their PARENT and CHILD under the supervision of the ADULT. (3) Ordinarily members err if they take group problems personally. If they do, they find it hard not to be defensive and find staying in the ADULT almost impossible. There are, of course, problems that are truly personal attacks, but members need to use this interpretation of the problem as a last resort, not a first conclusion.

SURVIVAL STRATEGIES

1. The best way to deal with difficulties in a group is to prevent them from arising.
   a. Help the members to become aware of the group process and the level of satisfaction it is bringing members early in the group life.
   b. Use this awareness to reflect on the workings of the group for a short period at each group session.
2. Be sensitized to the level of maturity of the group and behave accordingly, e.g., don't expect deep commitment/trust in yourself or others at the first meeting.
3. Leadership needs to be shared by all group members, in the sense that all feel responsible for accomplishing the task of the group and for maintaining positive relationships among group members. All are responsible for dealing with group difficulties. The "leader" who encourages this attitude and behavior will survive.
4. Handle each difficult situation with objectivity and empathy. Don't take problems personally. Don't try to solve difficulties all by yourself.

Summary

Groups have a life of their own, so it is not surprising that the difficulties they experience are different than we experience one-on-one in marriage, in friendships or in working relationships. In this chapter I have focused on some of these unique difficulties.

First, however, we surveyed some of the studies made in the last twenty-five years on group activity, the things that seem to go into a "good" group and some of the problems that can be anticipated in poorly constituted groups. Trust, communication and mutual respect seem to rank high in the group where few difficulties are found. Their absence creates difficulties in a "bad" group.

There are ways to prevent many difficulties from arising in groups in the first place. We can educate a group about those elements that need to be in any group to make it functional and to avoid using excessive energy and time on handling difficulties. We can anticipate and avert other difficulties by being aware of how groups normally develop and by being able to recognize stages of growth from immaturity to maturity in the group experience. We can also be sensitive to the style of leadership a particular group needs. We studied the different kinds of leadership that seem most effective in immature groups and the leadership styles that have proven effective in mature groups. We discovered that leadership is fundamentally a matter of making a sound judgment regarding the maturity of the group about whose leadership we are concerned and having the skill to fill the needs that the group cannot fill for itself.

The second half of this chapter dealt with individual difficulties that seem, to me, rather common to many groups. In the style of case studies, we looked at various situations that create group difficulties and at some strategies that have been found to resolve successfully difficulties like these.

While each kind of difficulty requires its own strategy of resolution, we also suggested some general rules or principles for approaching any group difficulty: (1) look for the occasion of the difficulty in the wider system, (2) stay in the ADULT, and (3) don't presume that any group difficulty is a personal attack.

Many suggestions about handling difficulties have been made throughout this chapter, as well as in the previous six chapters. However, because many people shy away from confrontation as a method of conflict resolution, I feel it useful to devote much of the next chapter on conflict resolution to the when, why and how of confrontation. It is not the only way to resolve conflict, as we have seen, but, at times, there are a very few alternatives to confrontation. We shall now broaden our perspective, reflecting on the use of confrontation in groups, in one-on-one situations and in personal relationships.

8

The Resolution of Difficulty

We have dealt with many strategies and techniques of resolving conflict in the previous chapters. There remains a "hard-nosed" approach in which we should also be skilled, at least for particular situations. It is *confrontation*. During a lecture in Baltimore, Maryland, some years ago, one of the listeners helped me to soften and to appreciate more fully the process of confrontation: "Everytime you said 'confrontation,' I thought of '*care*-frontation,' because you do not confront another unless you care about them." Perhaps she had heard this elsewhere, but for me it was original. I had felt it, but never articulated it. Confrontation is caring. If we don't care about others, if they are not important to us, we do not take the trouble to confront them.

A few years ago, when I directed an adult education center with dining and sleeping facilities, I had a waitress who was consistently hostile and sour. One of the objectives of our center was to create a climate of growth for all who came to us: teachers, executives, leaders, counselors, etc. Janet was not carrying our message as was needed. She was stamping negatives where positives were needed. I became concerned about her effect on our programs and about her. There seemed to be no other way to handle the situation than to confront her. Hints would not do the deed, or, at least, so it seemed to me. So, I confronted. The confrontation went like this:

Me: Janet, how have things been going for you, here at the center? How do you feel about your job—about the way the kitchen is running, for instance?

Janet: Yeah, it's O.K. I'm not unhappy.

Me: Are there any problems with Ike (the cook)?

Janet: No, he's his usual crazy self, but we put up with it. We've been with Ike a long time.

Me: Janet, I need to share something with you that seems to be having an effect on our programs. As you know (I could say this because we had regular full staff meetings that acquainted all staff members with the educational efforts of the center, as well as hospitality, etc.), one of our goals is to create an environment of growth and positive support here. My observations during the last few weeks have created some problems for me, and you are principally involved. You rarely smile while waiting on tables. Yesterday, at lunch, your attitude toward my table was almost hostile, so that even the guests at my table asked if anything was the matter. There seems to be a definite difference between your attitude and that of the other waitresses. And it's having an effect on our center.

Janet: I didn't realize that.

Me: I wasn't sure whether you did or not. Mainly, it's an attitude, never smiling, giving the impression that you're very unhappy with this job.

Janet: Well, maybe that's just me, the way I am.

Me: I can understand that to some extent, but we do need a more positive attitude here. I just want you to be aware of some reactions the people have to you. I wish you would try to be more pleasant.

Janet: O.K. I'll try.

Me: Thank you. That's all any of us can do.

As it turned out, Janet was one of our most loyal and enthusiastic employees. She remained in contact with me long after I had left the center, while I rarely heard from other former employees. She did make an effort to be more pleasant and I did not have to speak to her again during my directorship. In this case, confrontation seemed to deal with a simple lack of awareness, not with any deep-seated values or judgments. I had a sufficiently good relationship with Janet and the other employees so that I could confront rather directly and briefly. They knew I valued them and that I was deeply committed to our work.

Elements of Confrontation

My confrontation of Janet was not the best example of a classic confrontation. She was my employee, she was open to listening to me, and she seemed to recognize that I had no ulterior motives for the confrontation. All of this was in my favor. I know that such ideal conditions are not always present. There are times when we need to confront a peer or peers who are not open to hearing us and who suspect our motives. No question about it—these are serious issues in a successful confrontation. Because of them, confrontation might not be the answer to resolving our difficulty. When there is not a good relationship between the confronter and the confrontee, when trust is lacking and suspicion is present, confrontation might do more harm than good. In other words, you need to evaluate the situation, you need to think, before choosing to confront another. The question you need to answer to yourself is: "Is confrontation the way to handle this difficulty? Might I use a better approach?" In the next section we shall look at other ways to resolve difficulties, in addition to those we have already discussed in the previous chapters.

If we do choose to confront, we need to become skilled in four steps. (1) Create a climate of mutual concern, testing to assess the kind of rapport we have with the potential confrontee. If we cannot create a good climate or if we assess our rapport to be poor, it is generally best to avoid confrontation. Use another approach to the problem. (2) Clearly identify the particular behavior in the specific event(s) and be sure that the confrontee recalls the behavior/event(s). If the confrontee doesn't recall the behavior/event, do not confront. It will only conclude with the confrontee leaving you while thinking: "I don't know what he or she was talking about. I don't remember doing that"—and nothing will be learned or accomplished. (3) Help the confrontee to analyze his or her behavior in the particular situation(s) about which you are concerned. If he or she cannot analyze the effects of his or her behavior, make some suggestions and elicit his or her reactions. (4) This is the most important step: help the confrontee to learn from his or her past behavior, eliciting from him or her ways that he or she might act differently in a future, similar situation.

Creating a climate for confrontation. This means that we confront in a situation and environment in which we judge the confrontation will be successful. We need to ask ourselves whether emotions are too high to confront at the moment. Is it best to confront in the presence of others or in private? Is our relationship with the potential confrontee sufficiently good to handle the inevitable friction that comes from confrontation? Is the potential confrontee in a state of mind to handle a confrontation?

Creating the right climate means both making decisions about the immediate environment of the confrontation and about long term association with the potential confrontee. In the short term, we need to feel assured that all feelings are sufficiently controlled to handle confrontation without an uproar ensuing. We need to feel somewhat secure in our ability to handle the confrontee's reactions to the confrontation. For many of us, this is the factor that inhibits us from confronting. We feel we can "get through" the initial statement of concern. We aren't sure we can handle how the confrontee will react. Much of confrontation requires that our ADULT is firmly in control of our own feelings and behavior. Part of setting the climate is to trust ourselves. In the short term, also, we need to assess the disposition of the confrontee, assessing that we can make him or her feel fairly comfortable and open to the discussion. We realize that no one is ever completely comfortable in a confrontation.

In the long term, we need to assess our relationship with the confrontee. If it has been neutral or good, confrontation may very well be successful. If our relationship has been negative, confrontation is probably not the answer to solving our difficulty. In such hostile relationships each of us tends to hear only what we expect to hear. We tend to have heavy filters that look only for additional arguments supporting our negative attitudes. Communication is not likely until some preliminary defense-lowering has been accomplished. We need to repair bridges before we try to use them.

Identify the issue of confrontation. The issue might be the frequent behavior of the confrontee or an event in which the confrontee behaved in a way that proved difficult for the confronter. We can confront another over a value difference or over suspected bad intentions, but such confrontations usually are not successful. Confrontation is most successful when both parties can identify a particular piece of behavior about which the confrontation is to take place. In other words, confrontation is best used in references to what someone *does,* not in reference to what he or she values, thinks, intends or has been thought to think or intend.

We can confront another with little risk if the issue concerns some *strength* that the confrontee has but of which he or she seems unaware. This can be a pleasant experience for all concerned. It can also be pleasant to confront another *to encourage him or her* to take some action that the confronter thinks would be helpful to the confrontee. This can be helpful to someone trapped in indecision.

There is generally minimal risk in confronting another on *misinformation,* confronting to correct misunderstandings, errors or lack of information, unless the confrontee is one of our *definitely wrong* people described above on page 165.

When we think of confrontation, however, we usually think of confronting another on some *weakness* we perceive or on some *conflict we judge to be between what he or she says and what he or she does.* There is risk in both of these areas, but, approached correctly, it can be minimized.

After creating a climate conducive to confrontation and judging that our rapport with the confrontee can support a confrontation, we need to recall with him or her the behvaior that is causing us difficulty. As noted above, it is essential that we point out examples of this behavior and that the confrontee remembers those behaviors. It is equally essential that we approach this part of the process when we are in our ADULT personality level, never with anger or disappointment. If the

confrontee will not admit to the troublesome behavior, there is
no point in continuing the confrontation. Break it off gracious-
ly, with some statement like. "Well, maybe I'm mistaken, or
maybe we would do better to talk at another time. For the
time being, thank you for speaking with me." We can then see
whether such behavior repeats itself. If it does, initiate the confrontation as soon as possible after the event, when forgetful-
ness can be most unlikely. Our goal is not to "get the other" in
any kind of a game. It is to resolve a difficulty in a constructive
way. So, I do not suggest that you "lie in wait" for the next
"fall." Simply be observant enough to recognize the possible
continuance of the problem.

*Help the confrontee to analyze the effects of the confront-
ed behavior.* In this step of the process we want to reflect together on what effect the behavior had on others and, if
helpful and not too risky, what caused the behavior. A caution
is in order here. With this step it is possible to upset the confrontee to an extent beyond our capability to handle, particularly if we choose to examine the motives for the behavior.
Unless we are skilled in psychology, it seems best to avoid motives. Concentrate on the effect the behavior is perceived to
have had on the confronter or on others. Motives can sometimes explain and even excuse behavior, but it is best not to
probe too deeply.

First elicit from the confrontee how he or she saw the behavior, what effects it had, what were its consequences. Ask
questions like: "Was what you did helpful or not helpful?"
"What relationships do you see between our different views of
your action?" "How did you feel about what happened?" Only
after you have given the confrontee the opportunity to analyze the behavior should you make some suggestions, share
your feelings or offer your own opinion. It is best, of course, if
the confrontee analyzes as you would, seeing the behavior as a
source of difficulty. If he or she does not, however, it is perfectly acceptable to share your own feelings and the difficult consequences you perceive from his or her behavior. The goal of this
step is to perceive mutually how the behavior caused difficulty. If you are confronting on a strength, helping the confrontee

to see some competence he or she has, but of which he or she is unaware, the goal would be to perceive mutually how his or her behavior was helpful and skillful. *Help the confrontee to learn from his or her past behavior.* Again, do not make initial suggestions. Elicit from the confrontee ways in which he or she might behave differently in a similar situation in the future. Your goal is to help the confrontee to learn from the experience. There are some of us who have had "fifty years of experience," meaning that we have had one year's experience repeated fifty times. Confrontation is a caring modality, helping an individual to learn from each year of the fifty years.

Some questions we might ask, since this phase of the four step process is heavily dependent upon the confronter, are: "What does this suggest?" "What difference does this make for you?" "How would you act differently in a future, similar situation?"

An example of a classic confrontation follows. I shall illustrate the four steps of confrontation as we have discussed them. The situation involves a secretary who has been late on a job for a number of days over a period of two months. Jason is secretary to the vice president of the company. His associate, Tara, has regularly been late on Mondays and Wednesdays over the past two months. This has placed some pressures on Jason, since he has had to "cover for her" on these occasions. Jason has been patient, hoping for some explanation from Tara. He has given hints to Tara about the difficulty she has been causing him. Tara has offered no explanation. Their relationship has usually been good.

Climate: Tara is on time today. She is relaxed. Work is not pressing and the vice president is off to a meeting.

Jason: Tara, I need your help. I need to talk to you about some of my concerns. Can we talk now?

Tara: Yes, I think so. Why? What's troubling you?

Jason: I want you to understand that I truly appreciate your work and your readiness to give extra time when it is necessary. You're a good secretary and I like to have you as an associate. I think you know that.

Tara: I've always felt that you and I worked well together, but what did you want to speak to me about?

Identification: Jason identifies the behavior causing him difficulty.

Jason: I wanted to talk to you about your lateness a couple of times a week over the past couple of months—especially on Mondays and Wednesdays. Are you aware that lateness on these days is becoming a pattern? It's happened for the past seven or eight weeks.

Tara: Well, I know I've been late a few times, but I didn't know it had become an issue. What's your problem?

Jason: The problem is that I have to take the brunt of your absence. Most of the time you are late, I have to answer for it. Mr. Do asks where you are, and I have no answers.

Analysis: Jason continues the analysis of the consequences of Tara's lateness.

Jason: (continuing) Are you aware of the consequences of your lateness?

Tara: Well, I suppose I could be "docked" in my pay, if they made an issue of it.

Jason: No, I'm talking about how it affects me. As you know, Mr. Do doles out most of his correspondence as soon as he arrives in the office. I end up with most of the work of handling his letters. As a result I have little time to work on the "projects" he is always giving me.

Tara: O.K. I understand that only you can do the "projects." I don't understand most of them. But give me some of the correspondence, even if I'm late. I don't want to shirk my job.

Jason: That's the problem. You can't understand my shorthand. You've tried in the past without success. Unless you are here to take the correspondence, there's little chance of your

helping with it. Do you understand the problem you are causing for me?
Tara: Yes and no. I do wish you knew common shorthand,
but . . . All right, I am causing a problem. I'm sorry.

Learning. Jason pursues the confrontation, so that Tara
might change her behavior.
Jason: O.K. I know you did not intend to cause a problem,
but it's still there. Can you do anything about lateness in the
future?
Tara: Very little, especially on Mondays and Wednesdays.
I have to take my son to day care, and they do not open until
8:30 A.M. I can't be there and here at the same time.
Jason: Do you have any ideas about how we could handle
my problem?
Tara: Suppose I were to take all of the correspondence on
Tuesdays and Thursdays, leaving you free to handle the "pro-
jects"? Would that help?
Jason: That sounds like a real possibility. Let's try it. We
can talk in a week or so about how we're doing. I like the idea.
I foresee some problems with you getting the time to do filing,
but maybe you could concentrate on that on Mondays and
Wednesdays. Let's see how it works out.

This is an example of a classic confrontation—one that
works well within the confrontation structure. I grant that it
will not always be so. There are individuals with deep-seated
patterns and habits that they will find difficult to change. Some
have real "hates," "fears," "anxieties" and dislikes that are not
easily dislodged. This process of confrontation might have to
yield to more professional approaches. Our job is not to become more professional, but to recognize the limits of our expertise. We may try this approach of setting climate,
identifying, analyzing and generalizing. If it does not bring results, we know that we are probably "out of our depth." We
then need to make some choices. We need to choose to tolerate the difficulty, to elicit and/or encourage professional help,
or to use less direct approaches than confrontation.

If we choose to use confrontation, there is the non-verbal element to consider: our body language. Confrontation requires a certain amount of assertiveness. We need to act assertive, which means that we recognize our own rights as well as the rights of the other(s). We do not want to act aggressively, in the sense that we violate the rights of others.

Non-verbally this means that we sit, stand, and use our eyes in ways that say we respect the other but we also want respect for ourselves. If we sit, we sit straight, not slouching or in a submissive attitude. If we stand, we stand with equal weight on each foot, straight and without inclination. The message of forward inclination is "aggression"; the message of backward inclination is "submission." We do not want to convey either of these messages. Our message is that we are reasonable, caring and secure individuals who want our rights and needs respected, as we respect the rights and needs of others.

Eye contact can also convey messages that can help or hinder our confrontation. Too intense eye contact conveys the aggressive message that we want to subdue the confrontee. This will only defeat our purpose. Shifty eyes or avoidance of eye contact says that we are insecure or being deceitful. Hopefully we are neither, so we do not want to convey those messages. We need sufficient contact to indicate our sincerity and openness, without seeming to be an interrogator.

Other Approaches to Difficulties

In the previous chapters I have suggested various ways to handle difficulties, one-on-one or in a group: understanding differences, handling "Games," examining our assumptions and the possible assumptions of others, knowing ourselves, handling discounting, recognizing the source of the difficulty in a work situation, recognizing and handling our feelings, etc. These strategies, as well as confrontation, have been successful in my own experience. But there are still other approaches.

We can (1) withdraw from the difficult person or situation, (2) accommodate to the person or situation, or (3) collaborate or negotiate. How we handle a difficulty depends on its importance to us, the kind of difficulty we are encountering and the attitude of the person(s) involved.

Withdrawal is often the best solution to value conflicts. There is usually only a small possibility of resolving differences in values. Often the need is to recognize the conflict as a value conflict early enough to avoid involvement at that level.

If the issue is of no great importance to us, we also need to consider withdrawing. Confrontation requires considerable energy and caring, which we may not want to expend on an unimportant issue.

Doris, a neighbor of ours, is something of a perfectionist, which probably accounts for her business success. Having created her own business a decade ago, she has been fortunate enough to marry Matthew, a man who likes to shop, cook and do many of the customary housewife tasks. But Matthew's kitchen was never clean. Dishes would sit about for an hour or more after meals. The stove was rarely cleaned and the oven was scrubbed only when it began to smoke and smell. At first Doris was regularly upset, often doing the cleaning herself. Soon she found this too taxing, with her other responsibilities. She knew that Matt is a Perceiving Personality (Chapter 1), one for whom order and structure are not important. She appreciated all he did to care for her, so . . . "why cause trouble?" was her final solution. She tolerated Matt's different ways, recognized the unimportance of the issue and withdrew her attention. It only helped her marriage.

There are occasions, of course, when value differences or unimportant issues can be successfully confronted. Sometimes value differences must be confronted if a relationship is to endure, and values *can* be changed. It is only that they change with greater difficulty than opinions or behaviors. Also, issues that seem unimportant to some may be very important to others, and some resolution needs to be pursued. Withdrawal is a "solution" only when differences are too rigid or when they can be tolerated without much cost.

Accommodation is another approach to handling a difficulty. We can adjust our own thinking and behavior to "leave room" for the issue that is creating a problem for us. We perceive some value in what we have previously seen as a difficulty, and we allow ourselves to change sufficiently so that the issue does not continue to prove difficult for us.

My secretary Judy has been with me for a long time. When we first began to work together, I was new in the business of management. I enjoyed having a secretary at my beck and call. I would bring her into the office any time in the day to "take a letter." In time I noticed that filing was not being done, long term projects were never completed on schedule, and Judy was growing more irritable. We had a talk. She pointed out that she had no way of scheduling her day or her work if she had to respond to my "take a letter" throughout the day. I felt a bit affronted and restricted. "Secretaries should accommodate their bosses," I thought. But, on further reflection, I saw that she probably had a point. I have tried to accommodate Judy and the difficulty by limiting my dictation to an hour or so each morning, leaving Judy to set her own schedule for the rest of the day. I still would like Judy at my beck and call, but by accommodating I have a more efficient office. We get things done on time.

Collaboration/Negotiation can resolve a difficulty when both parties are feeling pain and an interest in solving the problem. Both parties are willing to work together toward a solution. This process of handling difficulty has some clear guidelines.

Before entering into collaboration both sides need (1) to be clear about what they want to achieve and (2) to be realistic about what they are willing to give to achieve it. They need to be sincere in their effort to come to mutual agreement, based on reason and free of any competitive behavior. If one or the other party is not clear about what he or she wants, he or she will be an easy victim to one of the "Games" we discussed in Chapter 2. If one or the other intends to give nothing in the collaborative effort, competition will usually replace collaboration. The fundamental assumption upon entering into collaboration is that we are dealing with reasonable, honest people.

During the collaboration/negotiation both parties need (1) to be open to other alternatives than they may have arrived at personally, (2) to be totally present with an awareness of their feelings, (3) to look at the "pros" and "cons" of proposed trade-offs, (4) to listen actively to the other, (5) to be able to recognize when additional information is needed for a solution and to delay any solution until the necessary information is gathered, and (6) to work to appreciate the perceptions of the other.

Juan, the director of a local social welfare agency, could not understand Mark, his assistant director. Mark never seemed to be in the office, and he could rarely arrange to confer with Juan when Juan asked for a meeting. Juan knew that Mark was a good social worker and he appreciated the talent and expertise that Mark brought to his job. But there was no communication. Mark liked Juan, but he did not agree with Juan's concern with paperwork. "A social worker belongs on the street" was Mark's favorite dictum. The difficulty surfaced during a routine evaluation of the department, both Juan and Mark receiving low ratings on their performance appraisals. Money, promotions and perhaps jobs were in danger of being lost. Both Mark and Juan felt the need to talk. They agreed to follow the guidelines of Collaboration/Negotiation, with which their training had made them familiar.

Before the session Juan was clear in his own mind that he wanted more communication with Mark, at least a weekly hour session, and that in return he was willing to let Mark make his own schedule as long as Juan knew where to reach him.

Mark decided, before the session, that he wanted less hassling from Juan and more help with his paperwork, and he would be willing to spend designated hours in the office.

During the session, the following happened.

Juan: Mark, I'm glad we could get together. I think the agency is doing well, but the commissioner doesn't agree. As you know, he feels that both of us could do better, and perhaps he's right. How do you feel?

Mark: Right now, not good. That last performance appraisal bothers me a lot. I don't know how you made out, but I was disappointed. I've worked my "butt" off in this agency.

Juan: I know you have. I didn't make out well either, so I thought we might work together on the problem, find out where it is and agree on some possible solutions. It might be good if we start out by sharing each other's ideas. I feel the need to have more frequent communication with you. I need to know what you are doing. I feel if I had that, I'd be more comfortable with the way you handle your job. You know that I want you in the office more.

Mark: I know you feel that way, but I became a social worker to be with people, and I think my place is on the street, where the problems are. But I do understand your need to have your assistant closer to you also. I'm willing to spend more time in the office, provided I don't spend it all on paperwork. I would like some help in that area, by the way.

Juan: You know we don't have the budget to hire any more people, Mark. It's really tight, and you know that. You do pretty well getting your reports in now, so I don't see how I can help there. Have you thought of any way to get help?

Mark: Well, I could commit myself to spend certain designated hours in the office. I could do some of it then, with the help of one of the secretaries.

Juan: The secretaries have enough work already. They really can't take on any more. But I do like the idea of your being available at specific times. Look, talk to one or another of the secretaries yourself. See if she could help. It's O.K. by me if she wants to do it.

Mark: I will. I haven't thought of doing it that way. I would have to spend more time in the office, but it would sure help my evenings. Right now I'm doing reports until ten o'clock every night.

Juan: How would you feel if some of that designated office time were reserved for a weekly conference between the two of us?

Mark: Yeah, I guess we do need that. But first I have to get a secretary to agree to help me.

Juan: All right, we don't have to come to any firm agreements in this one discussion. But I do need to meet with you weekly, however we can work it out. Perhaps you could come up with some time suggestions before our next meeting, after you've tried to get the help you need with the paperwork. I'd like to see you make your own schedule, making time for office presence and conference time, and I would appreciate being able to contact you during the day when you're on the streets.

Mark: That can be arranged, I'm sure. It'll just take a little more organization, but it'll probably be worth it. That was one of the things they criticized on my appraisal. O.K. Let me talk to some of the secretaries.

Both Mark and Juan came to the session prepared. During the session, the alternative of Mark soliciting help from a secretary emerged, an idea that neither had considered but both were willing to be open about. They seemed to be in touch with their feelings and truly heard what each other said. When Mark considered how designated office time might make his evenings freer, he was considering the "pros" and "cons" of a trade-off. Both recognized the need of additional information (that a secretary would help Mark) before firm agreement could be reached. Throughout, each seemed to try to appreciate the perceptions of the other.

The solution, under which both are now working, did not allow for Mark's desired secretarial help. He does spend designated time in the office, however, and this has reduced his evening work and provided conference time with Juan. Both men feel more comfortable and less as though they are working with a difficulty. Neither Mark nor Juan got all he wanted: Mark has no help with his paperwork and Juan cannot always contact Mark. These issues, however, do not seem to affect their performance or hurt the agency's work. Collaboration/Negotiation, in this case, seems to have solved the major difficulties. And, often, this is the most for which we can hope in any office, home or life.

Competition and *Cooperation* are also approaches to handling difficulties, in contrast to Confrontation. I have discussed these sufficiently in Chapter 5. They need to be kept in mind for the right situation. I mention them here only to complete the litany of alternatives to confrontation.

SURVIVAL STRATEGIES

1. Confrontation is a *learned skill.* Practice with small issues before tackling a major difficulty. Don't expect it to work all the time. Ordinarily it is one of the last strategies we use to deal with difficulty. Only rarely (such as when our rapport with another is the best) would confrontation be our first approach to resolving difficulty.
2. Remember that we can confront others on their good points. Confrontation does not always connotate stress.
3. Consider the different ways you could deal with a difficult person *before* taking any action. Don't use a hammer to attach a thumbtack or try to handle a hot pot with a single piece of cheesecloth.

Summary

When we speak about problems, difficulties or differences, we often think of arguments, the uproar that follows initial efforts at Confrontation. This chapter limits the boundaries of Confrontation, suggesting a process to confront without argument. We need to be as sure as possible about the time, place and relationships of the Confrontation. We call this "climate setting." We need to mutually identify the difficult issue, analyze it and explore ways to eliminate it in the future. Since the success of Confrontation lies largely with the confronter, we need to develop our skill slowly. At first, experiment with small Confrontations, practicing with issues and people that are likely to result in success. Adhere faithfully to climate-set, identification, analysis and learning. When we have had some small successes, attempt the larger issues that seem appropriate for Confrontation. It is most important to have initial success with the process.

Confrontation is not always appropriate. It is like the big hammer that can do more harm than good if used indiscriminately. Where issues are unimportant, not of sufficient concern to warrant the time and energy for confrontation, we may choose to withdraw ourselves from the issue. This means that we tolerate what we choose not to change. Even large issues, such as value conflicts, may be best to tolerate since there is little likelihood of changing them.

Or we may find it best to change ourselves to solve a difficulty. We may accommodate. In this instance, we recognize the validity of another's views and change our own behavior to meet our desired goals.

Collaboration/Negotiation is a useful alternative to Confrontation when the parties involved have mutual concerns but find conflict with each other in the pursuit of their common goals. Both parties need to have a vested interest in the outcome, be clear on what they want and what they are willing to forego, make efforts to appreciate and hear each other's point of view, be open to possible alternatives and be able to discuss openly the pluses and minuses of what they might need to give or accept.

Up until now we have discussed specific difficulties in life that can be aggravating. For most of us, they are found in the office, factory, business, home, relationships or neighborhood. There is a wider difficulty that touches our total life. That difficulty can be devastating. It takes different forms, but essentially it is a single difficulty. It is the difficulty of making life decisions: change of careers, job changes, divorce or separation, widowhood and remarriage. Such difficulties seem common in today's world and offer little promise of subsiding. We shall reflect on them in our final chapter.

9

Difficult Life Changes

Luke lost his wife last year. They had been married ten years, and she was only forty years old. He felt angry, then depressed, and, finally, he felt resigned. He still feels that life has stopped for him. His goals are vague and (he feels) unimportant. His difficulty is rooted deeply within the fabric of his life itself. It is not a question of handling a difficult incident or a difficult person. He faces a difficult life change.

Pasquale is divorced. His wife of twenty years initiated the proceedings on grounds that Pasquale could not overturn. Yes, he had been unfaithful and his infidelity had been documented. But Pasquale truly loved his wife and child. He never thought that his "playing around" would lead to a divorce. Pasquale is desolate, without sexual or any other appetite. He is in a difficult situation involving his whole life. He still has his job, but that is all he has.

Dee, age twenty-four, has just remarried. She was a teenage bride, marrying her high school sweetheart immediately after graduation. The marriage lasted two years and, for any number of reasons, disintegrated. She is determined not to repeat her failure, but the new marriage is not easy. It is too colored by her past experience. Dee is involved in a difficult life change.

Joel was a minister until five years ago, married with two children. At first he took part-time jobs to fill the gaps in his salary and family needs. The parish was unsympathetic, already overburdened with the expenses of maintaining the parish plant and staff. The council supported Joel's need to "moonlight," as long as the extra job maintained the dignity of

the ministry. Joel, with his Master's degree, took the job of directing a drug rehabilitation clinic. Soon he was offered a promotion that would prevent him from continuing in his
ministry career. He took the promotion, but he feels a nagging
regret that he can no longer share in the ministry for which he
prepared so long. He occasionally ministers on weekends, but
this weekend experience only increases his hunger for his first
love. He cannot return to the ministry without sacrificing the
stability and security of himself and his family. Joel is in a difficult life change.

At first Aaron reveled in his new-found freedom. After
twenty years of marriage, he found himself single. He had won
his divorce without any penalty. That was three years ago.
Now Aaron feels lonely, isolated in the midst of the "exciting"
singles crowd, wanting a stability he once had but has no more.
Aaron is trying to learn how to handle the single life. He is in a
difficult life change. He needs to make decisions, but there is
no one with whom to talk seriously. He is alone.

Shirley was a nun for ten years. She left the convent to
find a life of freedom that she could not find behind convent
walls. She resented being treated as a child. This was her perception and she sought a dispensation. It was granted. With
her education she soon found employment and developed
some relationships. But it was not easy. Shirley found the move
a difficult life change.

A "life change" strikes us at the root of our identity, of our
self-esteem and of our well-being. When we find ourselves
challenged in this fundamental way we can choose to change
our own behavior. We can choose to fit ourselves into the situation that we did not expect. Pasquale could have chosen to
stop "playing around." Dee could have chosen to work on
keeping her marriage intact. Joel could have chosen to keep
his family life within the confines allowed by the ministry. We
can also choose to change the environment of our life situation
so that we feel more comfortable. Aaron could have chosen to
heal his marriage rather than abandon it. Shirely could have
sought an assignment that allowed her the freedom she need-

ed while remaining within the religious life. Such choices are possible, if the situation allows.

But a "life change" may also be forced upon us. Luke had no choice. His wife died. If we are "fired" or "separated" from our job, we have no choice except to find a way to handle our new situation. In fact, it makes little difference whether we have a choice or not about our life change. Once we find ourselves in such a position, we need to handle it. Hopefully we will handle it in a constructive way. That is what this chapter is about.

Most of us are aware of friends who have chosen to change careers, or who have been forced to do so, for one reason or another. Physicians have chosen to become businessmen and lawyers have opted for livelihoods in real estate or the stock market. Ministers and priests have found themselves more satisfied in drug counseling, teaching or business. Unfortunately there are no hard statistics on such career changes. But I think most of us have a friend who has made this kind of choice or has been forced into such a choice. These are some of the people who face "life change." If it is forced, not chosen, it can be a difficult life change.

We do have firm statistics on marital changes. In 1979 (the most recent year for which statistics are available as of this time), there were 2,331,000 marriages and 1,181,000 divorces or annulments. In 1979, more than fifty percent of people involved in marriage found themselves in a difficult life change. In that same year, there were 582,000 remarriages, another difficult life change. Between 1975 and 1977, eighty-five out of every thousand women between the ages of fourteen and forty-four remarried; there were 1,508,000 remarriages during this period. As of 1980, there are 7,011,000 widows and widowers in the United States, a significant group who face difficult life change that has been imposed upon them. (Statistics from *Statistical Abstract of the United States for 1981*, U.S. Department of Commerce.)

In other words, there are many layers of life change. It can be *chosen* or *imposed*. It can be *lateral*, moving from one job to another of a similar kind. It can occur by a *promotion* or a *demotion.* Even a promotion can be a difficult life change. Or it can be a *total life change,* a change of career, of marital relationships or widowhood. Few of us escape life change, and it can often be difficult. Most of us need to reflect on its psychological impact and on its practical impact.

The Psychological Impact of Life Change

The most serious effects of life change touch our physical health. It has been more than fifteen years since Dr. Holmes, then of the University of Washington Medical School, and Dr. Rahe, then a neuropsychiatric researcher of the the U.S. Navy, joined forces to evaluate finds that they found difficult to believe. Difficult life changes seemed to have a consistent impact on tuberculosis patients, for the worse. The more change in life they experienced, the more likely they were to become ill. Holmes and Rahe began to chart the relationship between illness and the life changes that an individual experienced. They studied thousands of cases, but they waited for five years to share their findings, since they found those findings difficult to believe.

In 1967, when Holmes and Rahe released the results of their studies, a massive retesting project began. Subjects in the United States, Japan, Belgium, the Netherlands and France were tested. The results were always the same: too much life change over a short period of time brings on illness; in addition, the more extensive the life change, the more serious the illness.

Holmes and Rahe shared a rating scale with the world, suggesting a number of points that could contribute to stress in our life experience. When points mounted to 200 or so, we could expect some minor illness. If the points added up to 500 or 600, there would likely be a more serious illness.

Examples are:

Spouse's death	100
Divorce	73
Marital separation	65
Death of close family member	63
Personal injury/illness	53
Fired at work	47
Business adjustment	39
Change to different work	36
Home arguments	35
Change in living conditions	25

For the complete listing and instructions for evaluating see D. Dudley and E. Welke, *How To Survive Being Alive*, Doubleday & Co., 1977.

It seems to indicate that difficult life change is a threatening situation. We can handle only so much change in a given amount of time. No doubt this differs from person to person, but the threat is there. Those of us involved in a difficult life change need to be aware of the danger to us, both psychologically and physically. We are not superpersons. We have limitations.

Some of the suggestions that Dudley and Welke make are: (1) Become aware of those situations that place stress on us. Even vacations and holidays are stressful, according to Holmes and Rahe. (2) Recognize need to sensitize ourselves to difficult life changes, admitting that they have an effect on us that we have to handle. We cannot pretend that "it doesn't bother us." It does. (3) Consider ways to handle difficult life changes, ways to regain our balance, to make sense out of our lives and to be comfortable with ourselves. (4) Act on those considerations after you have taken your time to review them. Take your time. (5) Anticipate life changes and prepare for them in advance. Don't act precipitously and don't be taken by surprise. Be in control. (6) Don't allow too many life changes to happen at once. You are no different from anyone else. You cannot take too much change at once. (6) See your accomplishments as part of living. Don't take any accomplishment as a "stopping point." See the further possibilities, within the accomplishments or outside of them.

I think that all of us are surprised, at one time or another, by what happens to us. There are some things that are beyond our control: the sudden death of a spouse, a close relation or a friend. These are stress points we need to acknowledge. We cannot control them. We need to cope with them.

Other changes we can anticipate: retirement, business changes, beginning or ending school, school changes, making loans, holidays, vacations, etc. We can prepare ourselves for a career change, financially and psychologically, for a separation or divorce. It seems that it is only important that we recognize the impact such changes will have on us. We shall not continue as before. There will be new issues with which we must deal. How our ADULT uses our PARENT, as described in earlier chapters, is crucial during these times of difficult life change. We need some *caring for,* and we might be the only ones who can give it. We might very well need to PARENT ourselves.

PARENTING is largely a psychological experience: it is in the head. Try to zip the zipper on your child's jacket while you are thinking that you can't do it in that position. Then change your thinking. Tell yourself that you can zip that zipper in that position. I suggest that you will zip the zipper with your second attitude. Your PARENT is saying "You can do it" and you will. I do not adhere to the belief that you and I can do anything we conceive as possible, but I do believe that a positive mental attitude will accomplish more than we think is likely or possible. We need our inner PARENT to affirm our competence. I know it's strange. But it also seems true.

Phil, a football coach and friend of mine, felt burned-out. He read books on stress, but found little help. The physical and psychological indications of stress seemed alien to him. He enjoyed his work, took some pride in his accomplishments and wanted to stay in his profession. But he felt weak and without resources. He was tired. Things had changed for him. He was not in a successful season, he saw the road ahead to be steep, and he did not have the energy to go on. He quit.

Before Phil burned out he needed PARENTING. He spent too many hours away from his family, and, therefore, away from the kind of caring and support that all of us need. He needed a PARENT to discourage his "workaholism," and he needed time for himself. He made too many demands and changes on himself in every period of his life. He needed his inner PARENT to slow him down. Using only his CHILD (enthusiasm) and his ADULT (make money), Phil fell victim to changes that challenged and happened too quickly. He did not pace himself or his team; he unconsciously ignored the effects of rapid change and did not allow himself to revel in his accomplishments. His PARENT, had he listened, was saying: "Take your time," "Don't try to do too much," and "Enjoy your victories." Phil did not listen. He succumbed to a heart attack on a brief vacation. It may have been occasioned by the level of his life-style, which required a good deal of change and adaptation. We don't know, but Holmes and Rahe seem to make sense. Much of stress management training seems to have grown from their research.

The Practical Impact of Life Change

A difficult life change that is *imposed upon us,* such as widowhood, is, perhaps, as difficult as any to handle. Since it is imposed, and, often, unanticipated, it may be more difficult to cope with. Still, there are some guidelines that can be useful.

(1) *Be angry.* It's O.K. to be angry, especially when life has dealt us a "knockout punch." Perhaps some people would go down for the count. We are angry enough to remain standing, but we are "as sore as hell!" "It isn't fair!" And we are generally correct: it isn't fair. So we get angry. But we can't stay angry forever. I don't know of any instance where anger has replenished what I lost or made life more satisfying.

(2) *Be disappointed.* Be disappointed in yourself or in others. You expected more. Revel in that feeling for a while. It's

probably an accurate evaluation. We have the right to expect
more of ourselves and of others, but that isn't the whole story.
All of us have our limitations, the boundaries beyond which
our talents or strengths will not let us pass. Accept them, for
the time being, for ourselves and for others. Superman belongs
in the comic strips, as does Wonder Woman. Still, there is time,
and hope and another time. We can learn from mistakes. Only
genuine losers never learn from the past.

(3) *Be depressed.* You have lost something of value. You
have the right to be depressed. Probably what you have lost
cannot be regained. It is lost for this lifetime. You worked hard
to attain it and now it has been taken away. We don't need to
excuse our depression. But, again, what does it get us? It will
not return what we have lost. It will not provide an alternative
or a solution to our loss. Still, we have the right to our depression. In some strange way it helps—but never to the point of
hopelessness. We need to move beyond our depression.

(4) *Be resolute.* Depression can be helpful for only so long.
We need to turn to possible alternatives that can cope with our
loss. I know—the loss can never be replaced. The loss of a husband or wife is irreplaceable. We cannot, however, remain im-
mobile before a loss. If we do, the loss becomes compounded:
the loss of a loved one and the loss of the rest of our life. It may
not seem so, but we continue to be significant and important
in the swirl of life after a serious personal loss. We still touch
others. We may affect them in quiet ways, but ways that are
more significant than we think.

When I was eight years of age my grandfather died. My
grandmother had raised me between the ages of two and six.
With the death of my grandfather, my grandmother went into
seclusion. I had returned to my mother and father at the age of
seven, but grandmom was a significant person to me. She had
been there when I was sick for almost a year (it seems), and
now I saw her no more. It was a strange new world for me. I
felt "cut-off" and isolated. She never appeared again until she
was senile, at least as far as I remember in my young life. Then
she was a different person, a disappointment to me, a problem
to be dealt with. It was not until I was in my middle thirties

that I was able to regain something of a capacity of intimacy and caring for others. I grew up as a "loner," perhaps because I reasoned deep in my psyche that abandonment was the likely outcome of closeness. Grandmom never knew this, as far as I know, but her grief over the loss of her husband clouded over much of what she meant to others. I've never forgotten or, perhaps, recovered. The end result of loss is to live again. I wish Grandmom had known that.

(5) *Plan your life change.* There are persons and situations that receive such an abundance of help from others in a time of need that everything falls into place. For most of us going through a difficult life change, this is not so. We are left on our own. So what do we do? I suggest that we do what those who choose a life change do, what those for whom life change is not imposed might do to handle their new situation.

There are life changes that we choose, that are *not imposed upon us* by others. We can prepare for them, since we make the decisions that effect the change. There is still stress and the dangers of change that we have reflected upon above. Still, we retain a control that is heavily in our favor. We can plan. Whether change is imposed upon us or we choose it, planning is needed, sooner or later.

Most of us can divide our life into three levels of achievements and aspirations: *career, personal relationships* and *personal fulfillment.* We can look at these areas from the viewpoint of where we have been, where we are and where we would like to be. The ultimate question in our planning process needs to be with us from the beginning of the process. It has been best articulated by Dag Hammarskjöld: "What next? Why ask? Next will come a demand about which you already know all you need to know: that its sole measure is your own strength" (*Markings,* Alfred A. Knopf, N.Y., 1968, p. 129). Our planning needs to be colored by self-confidence and reason. We take responsibility for ourselves. Unlike Hammarskjöld, most of us need to ask what that means. It is possible for us to be consumed by unwarranted and unjustified demands. We need to reflect on what we need to make life meaningful. We need to decide where to use our strength, as long as we have a choice. The process sounds simple. From experience, I know it is difficult. We need to answer hard questions. Perhaps this is what makes a life change difficult.

Where am I now? Look at your career development to the present. If you are satisfied with it, consider how you can maintain your position. How will your life change affect your career and what are some ways to enhance the positive effects and lessen the negative ones. Or does your life change mean the end of your career? If so, and if the change has not been sudden and imposed, you need to plan a new career, new goals, new skills and ways to acquire those skills. Your age, status in the community and/or organization, family situation and personal inclinations all play a part in the planning process. And this calls for a good amount of self-knowledge. The advice of Socrates, noted in Chapter 1, holds true in handling any kind of difficulty: "Know yourself."

Personal relationships are an important dimension of this reflection. They may be few or many, but we need them. Somehow it is crucial for our physical and mental health that we have friends (family) with whom we can share at a deeply personal level. Surveys and research regularly surface this need. They also tell us that most real friends date back to school days. What we all know from the experience of loneliness is that the surveys and research tell the truth. In fact, we didn't need them to tell us this in the first place.

As we restructure our lives, we need to consider where we are in our personal relationships. If we have only acquaintances, we need to think about making some of those acquaintances friends. We need to question why we have so few friends, if that is the case. We may need to consider who are really friends, people who truly care for us and we for them, and who are not. As we think, we will do well to keep in mind that past wisdom has told us that we are fortunate if we acquire one or two real friends in a lifetime.

A successful career without someone with whom to share it is empty. Career and good personal relationships go together.

Personal fulfillment is another dimension of our present

consideration. Certainly a good career and good friends can mean a great deal of personal fulfillment. There may, however, be more than that we want and need. We may be a successful businessman or businesswoman with a satisfying home life and circle of friends. But perhaps we always wanted to be an artist or writer. A difficult life change can offer the opportunity for personal fulfillment. Our family is fragmented, or our business goes sour. Is this catastrophe or opportunity? Much depends on our health, our age and our determination. In the midst of a difficult life change, we may find an opportunity to be what we always wanted to be. I know, of course, that there are financial considerations. But the opportunity might be there.

I could write the stories of people like Abraham Lincoln, who suffered a nervous breakdown from a disrupted love affair, failed in business and tried for the presidency of the United States nine times before he found his place in life. Or I could describe Grandma Moses, or my own grandfather-in-law, who found personal fulfillment in sketching and painting only in their eighties. But we all know of such extraordinary people. We find it hard to identify with them.

Difficult life change usually happens later in life, when we have had the chance to develop some wisdom. Part of that wisdom should be to pursue what we have always wanted to do. In other words, a difficult life situation can be a time of opportunity in life. We need to look at what we have done and at what we have always wanted to do.

Where do I want to be? A difficult life change might find us exactly where we want to be in our *career,* in our *personal relationships* and in *personal fulfillment.* This is not unusual for persons in mid-life. After leaving a job or profession of twenty-five years, after losing a valued relative, a husband or wife, after failing in a long-term business, we are angry, disappointed and depressed. But we resolve to continue life and to plan again. We choose to build on losses and a solid past. We see the future as a new, if difficult, opportunity.

What is our career? Do we need more training? Where do we want to be in our career if we haven't attained that level as yet? Or are we satisfied with our progress? These are hard questions that we might have to face. Or is our career at its end? Do we need to adapt to that possibility? What does that mean for us personally and economically? Can we build on what we have done, or do we need to build on our hobbies, our interests, to initiate a new, perhaps more interesting, career? Or is our career still blooming? If so, what steps do we need to take to arrive where we would like to be?

There are equally hard questions to be asked about our personal relationships. A difficult life change can occasion the loss of friends and acquaintances. This is particularly true when friendships have been built around our work. But recent studies indicate that we find fewer friends when we are not only unemployed, but also when we change professions, have a death in the family (loss takes place gradually in this instance, at least very often), or when we are involved in marital disputes and divorce.

Personal relationships are so important to us that we need to maintain, rebuild or create them. Erich Fromm describes our urgency:

> The experience of separateness arouses anxiety; it is, indeed, the source of all anxiety. Being separate means being cut off, without any capacity to use my human powers. Hence, to be separate means to be helpless, unable to grasp the world—things and people—actively; it means that the world can invade me without my ability to react. . . . The awareness of human separation, without reunion by love, is the source of shame. It is at the same time the source of guilt and anxiety (*The Art of Loving*, Bantam Books, 1967, pp. 7–8).

We can choose to be alone, bitter and cynical after our loss. If we try this long enough, Erich Fromm suggests that we will grow insane (*ibid.*, p. 7). Fromm, an eminent psychiatrist, is not the last word. But many of use who have experienced a difficult life change find him to touch truth.

Personal fulfillment needs also to be projected into the future, unless our life change has freed us for personal fulfillment. Most of us need to look inside ourselves to find what we truly want to feel fulfilled. A career might do it for some. Healthy and real personal relationships will do it for many. I suspect, however, that a good number of us will find unfulfilled dreams and fantasies that are still possible for us—"things that we have always wanted to do." A life change can offer the opportunity to do them. The change can be difficult, but it can also be positive, expanding and live-giving.

Not every life change need be difficult, but many are. We have invested a great deal in the past. It is difficult to let it go. These are the kind of life changes I call "difficult." We can follow the guidelines suggested above and find success in the change. No guidelines, however, can make the transition easy.

SURVIVAL STRATEGIES

1. Be sensitive to your life style and life pace. Don't allow many changes to occur in a short period of time. If you have a life change imposed, control changes over which you have control. Keep an even keel.
2. Let your self go through the stages of a life change: anger, disappointment and depression. Don't fight it.
3. Recognize and accept your value in the face of a loss or defeat. Be convinced that you count.
4. The future is real. It is no less real because it is not the future that you envisioned or expected. Plan for it. Learn from the past to make a meaningful future. It may not be all that you want, but make the most of it. We may have only one go-round.
5. Accept support from others, even though "they don't understand." No one is an island. Never reject friendship.
6. Finances are important, but not overriding. Happiness does not come with money. Autobiography supports that relationships and personal satisfaction are more likely to bring happiness than money. Work to combine the human and the financial needs you have.

7. Age is important but not decisive. Live as you feel, not according to the calendar.

Summary

Millions of us are being confronted with significant life changes many of which we shall find difficult. How can we find a change that affects our fundamental life style, values and habits to be easy? We are what we do, and when we cannot do what we have grown accustomed to do, we find it difficult. It makes little difference whether the change is imposed or voluntary, lateral, a demotion or promotion, partial or total. A change that touches our very being is difficult.

There are strong indications that serious life change affects our physical health. A series of changes in life style, work, social behavior and personal choices seem, from extensive studies, to prepare us for serious physical problems. In the midst of these kinds of experiences, we need to *take care of ourselves* as we may never have done before. We need to PARENT ourselves. We recognize and appreciate our accomplishments, while feeling angry, disappointed, depressed and irresolute. Unless we resolve to continue to live and to achieve, we compound the loss, passing on to others a fear and anxiety that is not rightfully theirs. It is probably true that none can appreciate our loss. Still, it is our loss and we have no right to pass it on to others.

We can be angry, disappointed and depressed, while needing to be resolute and demanding. How long we remain incapacitated is up to us. Thousands of people have shown us how to handle the loss of a spouse, certainly the most threatening of losses. Often they were woven into the fabric of our lives, or they wanted to be. Nothing can make our choice of changing relationships with these close people a pleasant experience. Often, however, if we do not make the change, it is made for us.

We need to look into our career development, our personal relationships and our personal fulfillment. Life change can be an opportunity to develop and to grow in all of these areas.

Sometimes it is a mirror that suggests ways that we might act differently in the future. We may need to answer such serious questions as "Where are we?" and "Where do we want to be in a few years?" In a time of crisis, these are not academic questions. Their answers will determine our futures.

Selected Bibliography

Berne, Eric, *Beyond Times and Scripts,* Grove Press, NY.

Games People Play, Grove Press, NY, 1967.

Boyd, L.W. & H.S., "A Transactional Model for Relationship Counselling," *Transactional Analysis Journal,* Vol. 11, No. 2, April, 1981, pp. 142-146.

Brennan, R.E., *General Psychology,* Macmillan, NY, 1937

Davis, J.H., *Group Performance,* Addison-Wesley Publishing Co., Reading, MA

Dudley, E. & Welke, E., *How to Survive Being Alive,* Doubleday Co., 1977

Fiedler, F.E., *A Theory of Leadership Effectiveness,* McGraw-Hill Book Co., 1967

Fromm, E., *The Art of Loving,* Bantam Books, 1967

Hersey, P. & Blanchard, K.H., *Management of Organizational Behavior,* 2nd edition, Prentice-Hall, Englewood Cliffs, NJ, 1972

James, M. & Jongeward, D., *Born to Win,* Addison-Wesley Publishing Co., Reading, MA, 1973

Kahler, T. & Capers, H., "The Miniscript," *Transactional Analysis Journal,* Vol. 4, No. 1, January 1974

Levinson, H., *Emotional Health: In the World of Work,* Harper & Row, NY, 1964

Likert, R., *New Patterns of Management,* McGraw-Hill Book Co., NY, 1961

Schiff, J.L., The Cathexis Reader, Harper & Row, NY, 1975

Index